Holding Hands, Holding Hearts

Recovering a Biblical View of Christian Dating

Richard D. Phillips

AND

Sharon L. Phillips

P U B L I S H I N G

P.O. BOX 817 • PHILLIPSBURG • NEW JERSEY 08865-0817

Unless otherwise indicated, Scripture quotations are from The Holy Bible, English Standard Version, copyright © 2001 by Crossway Bibles, a division of Good News Publishers. Used by permission. All rights reserved.

Scripture quotations marked (NIV) are from the HOLY BIBLE, NEW INTERNATIONAL VERSION®. NIV®. Copyright © 1973, 1978, 1984 by International Bible Society. Used by permission.

Italics within Scripture quotations indicate emphasis added.

Page design and typesetting by Lakeside Design Plus

Printed in the United States of America

ISBN-13: 978-0-87552-520-4
ISBN-10: 0-87552-520-2

" 'What does the Bible have to say about dating? Nothing. And everything!' So write Rick and Sharon Phillips in this remarkably wise and careful book. They set forth a theology of dating and relationships, and then offer mature wisdom on how to put biblical principles into practice. The result is required reading for every single adult."

—Justin Taylor,
co-editor, *Sex and the Supremacy of Christ*

"A biblically based perspective on dating and relationships. If singles read and apply the biblical counsel of this book, many of the painful problems that couples might face after the wedding will be prevented."

—Wayne A. Mack, author,
Strengthening Your Marriage

"This book is for people who want to take relationships as seriously as God takes them. Rick and Sharon have a passion for redeeming romance and preparing both singles and couples for lives that glorify God. They take a marriage-based approach that honors the divinely designed differences between women and men. In biblical, practical, down-to-earth ways the Phillipses show how, by grace, love is really supposed to work."

—Phil and Lisa Ryken,
Tenth Presbyterian Church, Philadelphia

"Many single adults today are confused, disoriented, and frustrated with the dating scene. This terrific book brings clarity, a biblical orientation, and lots of hope."

—John Yenchko, co-author,
Pre-Engagement: 5 Questions to Ask Yourselves

"Finally, someone has provided biblically based, theologically sound, and practical guidelines on dating for singles. Rick and Sharon enable singles to identify and resist cultural trends that are so easily imported into the thinking of singles. I intend to require this book for my students for years to come."

—Dan Zink,
Covenant Theological Seminary

To the dearly loved singles of
City Light
Tenth Presbyterian Church, Philadelphia
1991–2002

Contents

Preface

THIS BOOK IS THE PRODUCT of many years of ministering to Christian singles. It is geared especially toward single adults rather than to teenagers. The material here is in some respects suitable for teenagers, given that it presents a biblical portrait of love. But in other respects it is less appropriate, since it assumes that its readers possess the maturity to enter into marriage and since we deliberately aim to help dating couples successfully grow into marriage.

We really began working on this book as soon as we began ministering to singles, through our counsel and prayers for so many who were struggling with frustrations in dating. Eventually, we developed a seminar that we continue to give from time to time, and that has grown into the material found in this book. We are pleased to state that we have never provided a seminar on this material without later learning that at least one couple straightened out their relationship and went on to get married. We have even had couples present us with children who were the eventual result of their understanding of God's teaching on relationships and marriage. (To our knowledge, though, none of the children were named after us!)

We have confidence in this material not because it represents our profound insight or wisdom—although we are encouraged by our experience in offering it—but because it rests on the inerrant teaching of God's Word. We hope it will shed biblical light on a subject that is murky to so many. We offer it with prayers that God will use it to the blessing of many Christian singles and to the glory of his name.

This book is dedicated to the singles of City Light from 1991 to 2002. It was one of the great thrills of our lives to pastor City Light, the singles ministry of Tenth Presbyterian Church in Philadelphia, where the two of us started our own relationship and where we were so inspired by the example of so many incredible Christians. We also thank Allan Fisher of P&R Publishing for his long-suffering patience as we worked on this book through the birth of several children, through a change of churches, and through a major relocation. We hope his patience is well rewarded. Above all, we give thanks to our Lord Jesus Christ, whose love for us is the foundation for any love that we will ever enjoy together. To him be the glory.

Introduction

"WHAT DOES THE BIBLE SAY about dating?" That is the question we set out to answer with this book. It was also a question we were asked by numerous young-adult Christians during our years in ministry to singles. It's a good question. It's the right question. It's a vital question that most singles need to ask before the far more frequent question, "How can I get a guy or get a girl?"

"What does the Bible say about dating?" There are two ways to answer the question. The first is, "Nothing." Paul never wrote a word about what to do on a first date. The Bible is not going to give you a direct answer about whom to ask out (or to whom to say "yes"). Furthermore, the very idea of his daughter going out alone with a single man would have driven the average prophet to distraction.

The question "To whom should I be married?" is as old as humanity, but the current notion of "dating" is a quite recent experiment in human relations. With this in mind, we shouldn't be surprised that the Bible doesn't give much explicit guidance when it comes to dating. The fact is that the Bible has no category for dating. If you look in your concordance for the words *boyfriend* and *girlfriend*, you aren't going to find anything. When it comes to male–female relationships, the Bible knows only three categories: parent–child, brother–sister, and husband–wife.

Dating is essentially a twentieth-century invention. But whether we like it or not, most of us who want to get married have to figure out how to date successfully. Even if dating is a worldly notion with which some Christians will be uncomfortable, it is nonetheless something that most of us can't simply kiss goodbye.

What does the Bible say about dating?
Nothing. And everything!
Our challenge is to think biblically
about an activity that isn't in the Bible.

The challenge before us is to think biblically about an activity that isn't in the Bible and that may expose us to worldly attitudes and behaviors. (This, by the way, is true not just of dating but also of work, families, and a whole host of other issues.) This is where our second answer comes in. "What does the Bible say about dating?" Previously, we said, "Nothing." There is no direct teaching on dating. But now we must answer the question by saying, "Everything!" That is, everything we read from Genesis 1 to Revelation 22 is of vital relevance to dating, as to all of life. We hope to show in this book that the Bible presents profound instruction and wisdom that may be directly applied to dating and that will help us to be blessed in dating relationships.

For instance, take what Jesus described as the two greatest commandments: "You shall love the Lord your God with all your heart and with all your soul and with all your mind," and "You shall love your neighbor as yourself" (Matt. 22:38–39). We need to apply those words more seriously to every aspect of life. In dating, this requires us to honor God first. Many Christians approach dating mainly in terms of pursuing romance and meeting their emotional needs. Far too few think of it as an opportunity to honor God and grow in grace. What about loving our neighbor? This commandment requires us to put our dating partner's holiness ahead of our happiness. If you are dating someone and the relationship does not grow into marriage, the least you can do as a Christian is to ensure that dating you was a spiritually beneficial experience.

When we make this type of application, we are speaking generally about how the Bible can speak to dating. But what about more specific teaching? For those of you who will marry or who desire to marry, the Bible provides the marriage relationship as the framework from which to consider dating. The approach of this book is to start with the biblical principles of a healthy marriage and to work backwards to describe a healthy biblical dating relationship. Now, a marriage proposal does not usually happen on a first date, nor would we advise that it should. But neither does a marriage really begin with a wedding. Whether we know it or not, the patterns we establish in dating continue into marriage. Therefore, the foundations for a healthy and godly marriage begin while we are dating.

Our approach is to take the biblical principles of a healthy marriage and work backwards to a healthy dating relationship. The foundations for a healthy, godly marriage begin while dating.

Think about the assumptions you currently hold about dating. You might even want to jot them down. To be obedient to God's teaching in the Bible, you'll probably need to challenge and confront many of those assumptions and beliefs. It is amazing how deeply and well hidden worldly beliefs and attitudes are in our minds. There could hardly be a topic more confused in our time than that of dating. As Paul wrote about life in general, we may especially say about romance and sexuality, "Do not conform any longer to the pattern of this world, but be transformed by the renewing of your mind" (Rom. 12:2, NIV). We need to have our minds shaped by the Bible rather than by the world.

Furthermore, the stakes are very high. More harm comes to many of us through dating than in any other way. According to the world, dating is a way for singles to enjoy the comforts and pleasures of the opposite sex. If marriage is in the picture at all, then dating is a tryout for a potential partner. The idea is to start living as if you were married and see how things go. If one isn't finding fulfillment in the other person, then you can simply break up and move on. It's not much different from finding the right pair of shoes. At least you can have some fun along the way, or so it goes.

The problem is that the heart doesn't work that way. The intimacy of romance—both physical and emotional intimacy—is one that binds two people tightly together. If we don't treat our own and others' hearts carefully, there will be a lot of pain and bleeding. A broken heart is no small matter, as so many of us know from experience. This is the cause of untold pain in our world today, and Christians need to respond to affairs of the heart with respect, with care, and with the wisdom that God is able to give.

According to the Bible's perspective, if you are dating you are not just holding hands, you are holding hearts. What you do with your own heart, and what you do with another's, is a matter of great importance. God's Word speaks clearly and powerfully: "Above all else, guard your heart, for it is the wellspring of life" (Prov. 4:23, NIV). If we really want to learn how to care for another's heart, God is willing to teach us.

> You're not just holding hands.
> You're holding hearts.

This book is organized into two main parts. Part One is *A Biblical View of Dating and Relationships.* This is a drama in three acts, which we will explore one by one: God's design in creation, the relationship fallen through sin, and the relationship redeemed by God's grace. In chapter 1, we will begin this story, and it is as great and relevant a drama as you will ever read, one that is intended to shape our whole way of thinking about relationships and love. Part Two is titled *Biblical Wisdom for Dating and Relationships.* Here, we will consider a number of important topics from a biblical point of view: attraction, first dates, commitment, and growing from dating to marriage. The book concludes with a chapter of encouragement for those struggling with contentment as singles, titled *Waiting for Love?* God calls us all to contentment and to purposeful godliness, and he gives grace for us to grow in character and usefulness in singleness just as in marriage.

Dating is one of the most important things we will ever do, and much rides on how we do it. For that reason, and as a man and a woman who once dated and whose hearts are now bound together in the covenant of marriage, we offer this book with prayers to God that it will inform the minds and bless the hearts of all who read it. We pray especially that as you learn from God's Word regarding this challenging subject, you will find practical help that makes a clear difference in your relationships. We dare to hope—and we have seen this hope fulfilled—that if you turn to the Bible for guidance and are humbly and prayerfully willing to follow in the path God lays before you, not only will you be more godly and loving in dating, but one of your relationships may ripen and mature into the blessing of a godly and loving marriage.

As we begin this journey into the Bible's teaching on men and women together, we should remember that we are not the first to struggle with this topic. Even wise King Solomon had his biggest troubles when it came to women. He wrote in Proverbs 30:18–19 (NIV), "There are three things that are too amazing for me, four that I do not understand: the way of an eagle in the sky, the way of a snake on a rock, the way of a ship on the high seas, and the way of a man with a maiden." Like Solomon, we can be greatly helped by turning to God for wisdom in the way of a man with a maiden, without losing any of the wonder that makes it so romantic.

PART ONE

A Biblical View
of Dating and Relationships

1

Love Made New

God's Design in Creation

IT WAS ALL SO GOOD. That's what the Bible says: good, good, good. The light was good. The plants were good. The water was good. But then, in Genesis 2:18, all that changes. Suddenly we read the words, "not good." Wouldn't you know that it had to do with a man and a woman coming together?

You hear this from guys all the time: "Everything was great until the girls got involved!" "Everything was going well, and then he got a girlfriend." To so many men today—including Christian men—women are the problem. But that isn't what God says in the Bible. When Genesis 2:18 says, "It is not good," God is talking about a man *without* a woman. The verse says—and this is where our biblical tour of dating begins—"Then the LORD God said, 'It is not good that the man should be alone.'" This is where we

start, with a man's need for a woman and with God's provision of a woman for the well-being of the man.

A Problem and a Solution

There were two ways in which God's observation was
true. It was not good for man to be alone, first, because
from the start God had intended for the human race to
consist of men and women together. This is what an earlier and vitally important passage, Genesis 1:27, teaches:
"God created man in his own image, in the image of God
he created him; male and female he created them." This
is the truest statement of women's equality with men!
When God made the human race to bear his own image,
he meant for that image to be expressed through the union
of a man and a woman. The idea of bearing God's image
is a rich and involved concept, but when we remember
that God is himself relationship, a triune God with three
Persons in perfect and eternal love, it makes sense that we
bear his image in part through loving relationship. So it
was not good for man to be alone because God's purpose
in creation envisioned a relationship. When God thinks of
man—that is, mankind—he thinks "male and female
together."

The second reason why Adam's singleness was not
good is more obvious to us today. It just doesn't work very
well. It wasn't good for him. Just as God looks in on the
average single man's life today—in his apartment, in his
refrigerator, and in his heart—and says, "This isn't good,"
it wasn't good for Adam back then. It wasn't good emotionally or spiritually or even physically. Adam wasn't
able to do the work that God had given him if he
remained alone.

"It is not good for man to be alone"—
emotionally, spiritually, or physically.

This brings us to a first important point when it comes to dating and relationships: God's regular intention for mankind is marriage. Under anything like typical circumstances, an adult man ought to be married. Given the way things are today, he probably needs to date someone. And it also means that when he dates, it should be with an eye toward marriage.

It is commonly accepted among men today that the great danger is to get married too early. The thought of marriage is approached with fear and trepidation, with the threat of what the man will lose mainly in mind. But in the view of Genesis 2—and in our experience in ministering to singles—the greater danger is what will happen to the man if he doesn't marry. It is not good for a single man to develop selfish and otherwise sinful habits. It is not good for a man to grow older without the sanctifying influences of a wife and children. It is not good for a man to battle with sexual frustrations. (The same things might be said about a woman, too, but the Bible is specifically talking here about the man.) What is good for a man is to seek a relationship that will blossom into marriage—the sooner in adult life, the better.

Since marriage is God's regular intention
for mankind, we should date with
an eye toward marriage.

You will often hear it said of a single person, "She's just looking for a husband," or "He's just looking for a wife." If you take out the "just"—as if that is all that he or she is looking for—then the Bible answers, "Good for her!" and "Good for him!" Marriage is God's regular intention for the blessing of men and women. There are exceptions (although if you are reading this book they probably don't include you), but this is the rule: "It is not good that the man should be alone."

This was Adam's problem in the Garden, and God didn't waste time working on a solution. Continuing with Genesis 2:18, God says, "I will make him a helper fit for him." The biblical narrative that continues is both fascinating and instructive:

> So out of the ground the LORD God formed every beast of the field and every bird of the heavens and brought them to the man to see what he would call them. And whatever the man called every living creature, that was its name. The man gave names to all livestock and to the birds of the heavens and to every beast of the field. But for Adam there was not found a helper fit for him. (Gen. 2:19–20)

Adam was alone and needed a helper. So God brought before him all the other creatures that he had made upon the earth. As lord of the Garden under God's overall lordship, Adam had the privilege to name each of the creatures. This must have taken quite some time, and it would have involved a great deal of investigation. After all, deciding on the name for something requires examining it and observing it in action. Adam was the first zoologist, studying each and every one of the beasts of the field and the birds of the air. Imagine the thrill of seeing a lion for the first time and deciding what to call this majestic creature. Think about the curiosity of first encountering a giraffe or an anteater, or the fun of playing with the world's first dog! Adam must have spent days and months, even years, engaged in this thrilling activity. He gave names to them all, each of God's wonderful creatures, as the Lord himself brought them by in a glorious parade. And yet, with that said, the conclusion to the tale is one of dissatisfaction: "But for Adam no suitable helper was found" (Gen. 2:20, NIV). The point was not a trip to the world's first and greatest zoo. The purpose had been to find a mate and companion for Adam, and none of all the animals that God had so far made fit the bill.

If that was true, then the Lord would just have to create something new, and this is what the Bible says happened: "So the LORD God caused a deep sleep to fall upon the man, and while he slept took one of his ribs and closed up its place with flesh. And the rib that the LORD God had taken from the man he made into a woman and brought her to the man" (Gen. 2:21–22).

Adam's opinion of God's handiwork is recorded in verse 23. Here, when the eyes of man were first laid upon a woman, out of his mouth came a great, resounding "Wow!" Here is the full quote: "The man said, 'This is now bone of my bones and flesh of my flesh; she shall be called "woman," for she was taken out of man'" (NIV). This is how the relationship between a man and a woman first began, and it wasn't a bad start.

A Suitable Helper

Adam is anesthetized, and his body is broken for the life of the woman. Woman is suitable for man because like no other creature she is really the same flesh and bone. Like Adam, the woman also bore God's image, and was made to enjoy the same fellowship with God that Adam did (Gen. 1:27). She received God's commands with the understanding that she held responsibility to carry them out (1:28). But if we stop here and understand *suitable* simply to mean *the same*, then we miss God's purposes for the creation of man and woman. After all, if the only goal were sameness, then God might as well have made another man.

But because of God's special purposes and the fellowship he desired for humans, he made woman distinct from man. Her differences provided the perfect complement to Adam. This tells us something about what God wants. "God is love" (1 John 4:8), and God wants Adam to know what it means to love. Therefore, God created the woman, who was made of Adam but differently, so that Adam would know a love that was more than self-love.

The fact that men and women are different is not a curse or the product of sin. God made us this way. But that is not how many of us think. "If only women were just like guys," men lament (and vice versa). In Adam's world not marred by sin, this distinctiveness was not a source of frustration but a delight. Rather than have Adam bear the burden of God's purposes alone, God provided a helper with whom Adam could labor. The woman was not given to replicate the activities of man, but as a helper she complements and completes Adam in the work that they are now both assigned by God (Gen. 1:28). They were told to rule, to subdue, and to be fruitful and multiply.

That men and women are different is not a curse or a product of sin. God made us this way.

24

The woman was not merely different from Adam; she was "suitable" or "fit" for him. They fit together the way two pieces in a jigsaw puzzle do. This is evidenced by Genesis 2's comparison between the animals and birds and the woman whom God made from Adam's own flesh. Walter Wangerin has explained this concept particularly well:

> Beasts of burden conform to their owner's desires, bearing the drover's loads, plowing the farmer's fields . . . This sort of creature and this sort of relationship, is not "fit" for a spouse.

> Birds fulfil the aesthetic side of the human's superior nature, beautiful in their plumage, thrilling in their song, the focus of human dreams to fly, to soar, to be free of this drudge existence. But neither is a spouse "fit" only to be a beautiful object, a lovely but idolized thing, a "hunk" to show off, or a gracious goddess who satisfies my sense of my own importance.

> And cattle are considered personal property—the domesticated animals of Genesis. In fact, the word *cattle* is a cognate of the words *chattel* and *capital*, as in "capital gains." Animals may be the possession of another human being, but a spouse was never meant to be.

> The slow may make up speed by riding horses so the horse is a help. The weak may make up strength by driving oxen; so the ox is a help. The blind use dogs. The thirsty milk cows; the hungry keep hens and slaughter steers; the sentimental fix affection upon cats. Humankind has always made up its lack of skills in the skills of animals. But that purpose . . . is not fitting for a marriage and is dangerous wherever it is

found, because it reduces the spouse's role to that of an animal—something to be used.[1]

These comparisons may give us some insight into why some women chafe at the idea of being made as a *helper* for a man. In a fallen world such as ours, the word *helper* can be misunderstood and abused. It often has negative connotations of something weak, extraneous, and devalued. In a postmodern world riddled with the battle between the sexes and a well-entrenched struggle for equality, one might be accused of oppressing women by even alluding to this truth. Some reading this might argue that women have come too far to lower themselves to being men's helpers. "What have we done to deserve this? This is a biblical truth we cannot accept," some assert.

Let's put those conceptions aside and take a fresh look at the meaning of the text. The Hebrew word for *helper* is *ezer*. What is said of how woman will function in relationship to man is also said of God as the *Ezer* of Israel. God was a help to Israel most powerfully as Jehovah God, their Redeemer. As helper, he powerfully delivered Israel from their enemies. On one occasion he is called *helper* when he gently fed a prophet, a widow, and her son; this is again said of God when he was a patient shepherd to Israel in the wilderness. Psalm 121 puts it in especially beautiful language: "I lift up my eyes to the hills. From where does my help come? My help comes from the LORD, who made heaven and earth" (vv. 1–2). We could continue with the examples, but you get the point. To call a woman a helper is not to emphasize her weakness but her strength, not to label her as superfluous but as essential to Adam's condition and to God's purpose in the world. *Helper* is a position of dignity given to the woman by God himself.

> To call a woman a "helper" is to emphasize
> not her weakness but her strength.
> It is a position of dignity given by God himself.

Genesis 2:20 says that God made Eve because no suitable helper was found "for Adam." The woman, therefore, was created for the man (see 1 Cor. 11:9). Here again, many women (and some men) will cry out in anger: "Isn't it archaic to believe that woman exists for man?" The loudest message today is the one that says, "I am created for myself, for my own personal fulfillment and happiness." But the Bible says that we were all created for others, and especially for God's glory (see Rom. 11:36). "But won't I be confined to having no initiative; won't I be taken advantage of, used, and thrown away whenever the man feels that I have lost my usefulness to him?" God does not intend that a woman should be so used. Matthew Henry helps us to see God's purpose with greater clarity. He writes of God's gift of the woman to the man: "The woman was made of a rib out of the side of Adam; not made out of his head to rule over him, nor out of his feet to be trampled upon by him, but out of his side to be equal with him, under his arm to be protected, and near his heart to be beloved. Adam lost a rib . . . but in lieu thereof he had a helpmeet for him, which abundantly made up his loss."[2]

> The woman was made out of a rib: not out of
> his head to rule him, nor out of his feet to be

trampled by him, but out of his side to
be equal with him, under his arm to be
protected, and near his heart to be loved.

It may be helpful at this point to understand rightly Adam's position and calling in the Garden. Adam and Eve were together called to exercise dominion over the creation (see Gen. 1:28, which gives this authority "to them"). But Genesis 2:15 makes it clear that Adam in particular was granted lordship in the Garden, under God's ultimate sovereignty. The New Testament consistently looks back on the events of the Garden to establish the principle of male leadership in the home and in the church (see 1 Cor. 11:3 and 1 Tim. 2:12–14). But we make a great mistake if we understand Adam's lordship to emphasize his privileges. Instead, Adam's lordship was one of obligation.

This comes through especially in the tasks assigned to Adam in his lordly office: "The LORD God took the man and put him in the garden of Eden to *work* it and *keep* it" (Gen. 2:15). This verse contains two key verbs. The first is the Hebrew *'abad*, which is elsewhere used in the context of priests' ministry among the people and which here has an agricultural connotation. It speaks of a ministry of cultivation and nurture. So Adam's lordship was to take the form of nurturing. How directly this confronts the view of our society that men should be stoic and unfeeling! Adam's first calling was to make things grow and blossom, and in our relationships this is true of the hearts of those to whom men minister. The second verb is the Hebrew *shamar*, which means to guard or protect. So Adam's lordship was to take the form of nurture and protection. Adam was called to a servant-lordship.

> Adam's lordship was to take the form
> of nurture and protection. Adam was
> called to servant-lordship.

If the woman was created as a helper for the man, this is not to say that she alone was called to servanthood. She was the servant-helper and Adam was the servant-lord. Both are to be servants in complementary ministry according to God's design. How beautiful this all appeared in the pristine glory of the Garden before the entry of sin into the world! If sin has made God's arrangement offensive to us, the answer is not to reject his design but to have it redeemed in Jesus Christ. To say that the woman was made for the man is not to demean her but biblically to define her ministry in relationship to the man. This is not her only relationship and often not her only ministry; especially significant is her own relationship to God and her calling to serve him with her gifts and talents.

Moreover, the woman was given to man not for his whims but for his character. A woman does not find her fulfillment by supplanting a man in his God-given role of exercising lordship in the creation. Rather, she elevates a man in true masculinity; it is no understatement to say that it takes a woman to make a real man. In a perfect paradise not touched by sin, God's people delighted in his design. *Helper* was not a position for Eve to fight, but a function for her to fulfill. It is God's design, bearing his fingerprints for his glory and our good, a design we tamper with at our own peril. As the man delighted in the woman, so also she delighted in her calling and fully embraced it. This is why she is called his "glory" (1 Cor. 11:7).

A woman was given not for a man's whims
but for his character. She elevates him
in true masculinity. It takes a woman
to make a real man. This is God's design,
and we tamper with it at our peril.

The result of God's design was perfect companion-ship. Adam and Eve were like two sides of the same coin. She really was exactly what he needed, a suitable helper. People talk about a dog being "man's best friend." But a dog cannot share a man's dreams, cannot kneel beside him in prayer, cannot exhort and encourage him with God's Word, and cannot inspire in him the self-sacrificing love that makes him godly. The same might be said of male friendships. Too many Christian men rely on their male relationships for spiritual support, when what they most need is a godly woman. A woman was made to fit with a man: to match his strength with her resilience, to minis-ter to his heart with the power given to her by God. Only a woman is a suitable helper for a man.

If men need women, the same is true in the opposite direction. A woman who rejects God's design as a helper in the life of a man loses much of what makes her a woman. What is left for her but to take her place in "the man's world"? This does not mean that women may not have important positions or undertake meaningful careers. We should always remember that the first thing said about women in the Bible is that they are made in God's image, just as men are, having the service of God's glory as their highest calling. But as the very name "woman" suggests, she was formed in relation to man. She brings beauty into the world for him. She ministers to him in light of the struggles and trials of his life. She stands beside him. She makes demands on him that God intends for him to fulfill. Without her, things are "not good" for man; without him, she loses an important part of her identity and calling. Only after the woman had been made from the man and given into Adam's waiting arms could the Bible finally say, "God saw all that he had made, and it was very good" (Gen. 1:31, NIV).

> A woman who rejects God's design as a helper in the life of a man rejects much of what makes her a woman. What is left but to take her place in "the man's world"?

Building Blocks for a Marriage Relationship

How does this presentation of God's design for marriage relate to single men and women today? Does this simply add to the chorus that singles have no life until they get married? Not at all. As we have already said, there are exceptions to the rule that God's regular pattern for our blessing includes marriage. Furthermore, like Adam before Eve, even apart from marriage we are not really alone because of God's companionship with us. The most important relationship in every Christian's life is his or her relationship with God. Singles can be content and should be purposeful in their service to God. But if we are going to biblically understand the relationship between men and women, we simply must start with the way God made things. If Genesis 1 and 2 present God's purpose in marriage, and if our view of dating is directed toward marriage, then this tells us not only what we are aiming at but also much about how to build a relationship in that direction.

To that end, we turn to the concluding verses of Genesis 2 and find some key biblical commentary on the man and the woman together in marriage. According to verses 24–25 (NIV), "For this reason a man will leave his father and mother and be united to his wife, and they will become one flesh. The man and his wife were both naked, and they felt no shame." Not only is that a beautiful statement of what it means to be united in marriage, but it tells us much about the kind of relationship marriage involves. Before departing our study of this key chapter, we should observe three dynamics that bind the man and woman together in marriage and serve as building blocks for growing a healthy dating relationship: commitment, intimacy, and interdependence.

The first of these dynamics is *commitment*. This is an absolutely necessary component of any relationship like Adam and Eve's. For the sake of a woman, "a man will leave his father and mother and be united to his wife, and they will become one flesh" (Gen. 2:24, NIV). This—to leave and "cleave," as the King James Version puts it—is what commitment is all about, and a dating relationship that is moving toward marriage will have more and more of it over time. Commitment involves cleaving, that is, uniting together in a new relationship. As a dating relationship grows, more substance will develop in it, and the man and woman will each have more of themselves in the relationship. What does commitment involve? It involves an increasing exclusivity in terms of relationships with others; it means giving time to the relationship; and it involves a growing attention to the needs of each other.

At the start—on a first date—commitment is low. The couple is not likely to be dating exclusively, there is little expectation for each to give time to the other, and, while they should certainly seek to be a help and blessing to each other, their obligation is little higher than that toward any other brother or sister in Christ. By the time they have married, how much this has changed! The man is completely committed, loving his wife as Christ loved the church (Eph. 5:25) and practicing the kind of self-sacrifice for her that Jesus showed us on the cross. The woman is no less committed, submitting herself wholly to the authority of the man as the church submits to Christ. Between a first date and a wedding, this commitment must grow if the relationship is to flourish.

Cleaving involves *leaving*, of course. As commitment increases, parts of the old life must be left behind or adjusted. The man will watch less sports on television, while the woman will spend less time on the phone with friends. Their reliance on family and friends will be left to make room for their mutual reliance in the new relationship. Old priorities and allegiances give way to the growing partnership of the man and the woman.

Many singles today, especially men, flinch when it comes to commitment. They want to enjoy the new relationship without giving up anything from their former lives. They especially fear to close the door on other options in order to "settle for" a sole mate. But what they are turning their back on is love as God designed it between a man and a woman.

Commitment is realized through *faithfulness*, one of the most glorious of God's own attributes. God wants Christian men to be faithful, and in no relationship on this earth is this more demanded and developed than in a man's relationship with a woman. To safely enjoy the blessings of love with a member of the opposite sex, we must be willing to assume expectations and obligations that go with the relationship. A dating relationship that is growing toward marriage is one in which the man and the woman grow in confidence toward each other as expectations and agreements are faithfully met.

Commitment is realized through faithfulness, one of God's most glorious attributes. Between a first date and a marriage, commitment must grow.

The second dynamic of the marriage relationship described in Genesis 2 is *intimacy.* Genesis 2:24–25 (NIV) says that the committed couple "will become one flesh." It says of Adam and Eve, "The man and his wife were both naked, and they felt no shame." It is in this capacity for intimate union that a man and woman are so suitable as companions for each other. Men and women are made of the same substance, they equally bear God's image, and they are called into a common purpose and labor to the glory of God. Men and women are made to fit together for the most intimate ministry one to another—spiritually, emotionally, and physically.

It is because men and women can become so deeply bonded together, and because the breaking of these bonds does so much damage, that commitment is so necessary for healthy intimacy. This is why God's restriction of sexual intercourse to marriage is for our protection, because any other relationship lacks the commitment needed to make it safe for our hearts. If you doubt this, then glue two pieces of paper together and then try to separate them. To pull them apart there will be ripping, and the same is true for couples united emotionally and, especially, sexually. Their hearts have become one, and they cannot be casually separated. Moreover, intimacy involves uncovering and exposing oneself: "They were naked." Especially in a sinful world such as ours, one is foolish to expose the secrets of his or her heart to someone who has not made a tangible commitment to faithfulness. Intimacy should therefore follow commitment; commitment is the cup into which intimacy is safely poured and from which it is wholesomely enjoyed.

If commitment is fulfilled through faithfulness, intimacy is realized through *sharing*. A man and a woman share their hopes and dreams, their pasts and their futures, their burdens and their cares. What a wonderful blessing it is to have a suitable companion with whom you can share your fears, your pain, your passions, and your delights. As a dating relationship grows toward marriage, an increasing amount of sharing will take place between the hearts and minds of the couple.

> Intimacy is realized through sharing. Intimacy follows commitment; one is foolish to expose the secrets of his or her heart to someone who has not committed to faithfulness.

Third, the marriage relationship involves *interdependence*. The man and the woman are not just two people doing their own thing. They are a team, working in concert. Neither can succeed in his or her calling without the contributions and involvement of the other. The most graphic instance has to do with childbearing. Paul writes,

"As woman was made from man, so man is now born of woman" (1 Cor. 11:12). But this interdependence applies to all of a man and woman's life together. Therefore, for a dating couple to grow toward marriage, they must learn how to work together. This does not always mean that they share exactly the same tasks. Instead, they will learn to appreciate and complement their differences, to uphold each other in prayer, and to communicate effectively with regard to shared goals. They would be wise to serve together in ministry. Interdependence is achieved through *teamwork*, which is the ability to work as one.

> Interdependence is achieved through teamwork, the ability to work as one.

Commitment, intimacy, and interdependence—these are the building blocks by which a healthy dating relationship grows toward marriage. They start out small—a first date does not and normally should not involve a great deal of commitment, intimacy, or interdependence—but as a couple desires to grow toward marriage, they should pray for these qualities to grow in their relationship and they should give of themselves along these lines. This is, by the way, the best way to develop a healthy marriage. A strong marriage draws from the relationship that was developed before the wedding, a relationship that grew according to the architectural plans of God's design in creation.

2

Trouble in Paradise

The Relationship Fallen in Sin

IT IS HARD FOR US TO IMAGINE what it was like for Adam and Eve in the paradise Garden, but they must have had a beautiful relationship. There was no sin to cloud their love. There were no arguments or petty games. With their pure hearts, they would have known an intimacy no longer possible to people like us, who always have something to hide and can never fully let go of selfish motives and sinful desires. "The man and his wife were both naked and were not ashamed" concludes the biblical description of the first romance (Gen. 2:25). That is a remarkable statement of the ideal love relationship, one in which all the barriers are down and all is good.

Another way to measure the glory of Adam and Eve's marriage is found at the beginning of Genesis 3. Here we learn of the enemy of God who lurks in the Garden, the crafty serpent—Satan, the fallen archangel determined to ruin and conquer God's perfect world. Genesis 3 records his plan to oppose the Lord, and it is worth noting where he directs his attack—at that union of man and woman that rests at the pinnacle of God's creation. The devil's attack against God begins with the greatest of God's creatures, the one who has dominion over all else, the one who bears God's image and holds the dearest place in God's heart. It says quite a lot that what the devil hated most in God's perfect world was the man and the woman in their relationship with God.

Why is love so hard between a man and a woman today? The answer is found in Genesis 3. The problem with our relationships is sin. Sin and its outworkings bring so much misery and frustrate our hope for the blessings of love.

> Why are relationships so hard today?
> The answer is found in Genesis 3.
> The problem is sin.

The Fall

Genesis 3, one of the darkest chapters in all the Bible, tells the story of how the devil brought sin into the marriage relationship. The devil's offensive was cleverly conceived. The way to destroy Adam and Eve, he realized, was to turn their hearts away from God. He did so by first deceiving the woman, persuading her to desire and then to eat from the forbidden tree of the knowledge of good and evil. Now he had Adam in a dilemma. Adam was faced with a choice possible only in a world where sin has entered. He must, he thinks, either obey God and lose his beloved Eve or enter with her into rebellion and lose his own standing before God. The choice was between the gift and the Giver, between Eve and the blessed Creator. "He ate it," Genesis 3:6 (NIV) tells us of the fruit held forth by the hand of Eve, Adam's helper, and his choice was irrevocably made.

Adam was wrong, of course. We do not have to choose between the gift and the Giver. Satan had been using Eve to get at Adam. Instead of turning in faith to God for help, Adam turned away from God, and that is why he fell into sin.

Some important points can be made here regarding the nature of sin. Sin is the rejection of God's authority. Sin is based on a denial of God's goodness and truth. Sin involves idolatry. In this case, Adam gave Eve the place in his life reserved for God alone. He made her the ultimate object of his worship; now that Adam had turned from God, she would have to be the source for blessing in his life. Eve was not designed to do this. She was made to be a suitable helper for him, not a goddess.

> Sin is the rejection of God's authority, a denial of God's goodness and truth. Adam sinned by worshiping Eve in the place of God.

By turning Adam and Eve away from God, Satan undermined the foundation of their relationship to each other. God was the true foundation for their love, and now they had rebelled against the Lord. The devil had promised them, "You will be like God" (Gen. 3:5). But that was a lie, and they, like so many others after them, would find that no human being is able to meet our needs and make us happy. We may play at God, and we may look to one another to provide blessings that only God can give. But as the aftermath of Adam and Eve's sin shows, their rebellion against God ruined the love that God had intended them to enjoy. To this aftermath we now turn.

Fig Leaves and Pointed Fingers

Adam and Eve's fall into sin is a great turning point in the Bible and in the history of our race. It is also a significant turning point in terms of understanding the relationship between men and women. So much of what men and women struggle with today can be seen right here in Genesis 3; indeed, to biblically understand the problems that sin brings into our relationships, we need to pay careful attention to what happened next.

The first effect of sin was alienation. The man and the woman could no longer be in fellowship with God. Furthermore—and this might have come as a surprise to them—they could no longer enjoy their previous fellowship with each other. They were no longer pure, no longer innocent. Genesis 3:7 tells the tale: "Then the eyes of both were opened, and they knew that they were naked. And they sewed fig leaves together and made themselves loincloths." Gone were the days of shameless and open disclosure; Adam and Eve now had something to hide, something to cover up, something wrong at the core of their beings. They were no longer right with God, and so they could no longer enjoy the same kind of intimate love for each other.

The first effect of sin was alienation:
the man and the woman could no longer be

40

in fellowship with God, nor could they enjoy
their previous fellowship with one another.

Before long, God entered the scene, and the result of
sin was now shown in all its tragic consequences:

> And they heard the sound of the LORD God walking in the
> garden in the cool of the day, and the man and his wife
> hid themselves from the presence of the LORD God among
> the trees of the garden. But the LORD God called to the
> man and said to him, "Where are you?" (Gen. 3:8–9)

Adam responded to God's question by saying, "I heard
the sound of you in the garden, and I was afraid, because
I was naked, and I hid myself." The Lord replied, "Who
told you that you were naked? Have you eaten of the tree
of which I commanded you not to eat?" (vv. 10–11).

Worth noting is the tree from which God commanded
Adam not to eat. It was the "tree of the knowledge of good
and evil" (Gen. 2.17). We live in an age that says new experiences will set us free, that if we remain shackled into a
narrow life we will shrivel and shrink. But how different
is the reality when it comes to sin! The knowledge of sin
through experience is not a blessing. The only things Adam
gained from the forbidden fruit were the guilt of his sin
and the loss of his relationship with God. Now, in sin,
nakedness was a source of shame and the presence of the
holy God was a threat to him.

Adam was no longer at peace with himself and no
longer at peace with God. But at least he had Eve. That is
the attitude of so many today: "I don't need God and I don't
need to be made whole—all I need is someone to love."
The problem is that this, too, was lost. God inquired, "Have

you eaten of the tree of which I commanded you not to eat?" (Gen. 3:11). Notice Adam's tragic reply: "The woman whom you gave to be with me, she gave me fruit of the tree, and I ate" (v. 12). This was true, of course, but that is not the point. Adam was the first blame-shifter, and the first of a long, long line of men to put down his wife for his own sin. Given two hands by God, Adam used each of them to point a finger. "The woman," he cried, pointing at Eve, "you put here with me," pointing the other at God.

What a pathetic portrait of what sin does to a once-noble man! "It's not my fault!" Adam cries about his own sin. Desperate to remove the guilt from himself, with sin now brimming in his heart, he attacks the woman he once so adored. Things are only slightly better when we turn to Eve. God demanded of her, "What is this that you have done?" She replied truthfully, although not fully, "The serpent deceived me, and I ate" (v. 13).

"What is the problem with relationships?" so many people ask. Here it is: sin. When we considered God's design of the marriage relationship, we talked about the three dynamics of commitment, intimacy, and interdependence. This is the architecture of a strong relationship and the building blocks that a dating relationship should develop. All of these are distorted and twisted by sin.

Look at what sin does to commitment; Adam's commitment to Eve is traded for a self-centered concern for himself. What about their glorious intimacy? They had been naked and without shame. Now? Sin corrupts intimacy with shame and offers secrecy in its place. The same effects are seen with regard to interdependence. Because of sin, conflict now reigns. How profound and relevant is the Bible's presentation of sin! These are our very problems today; this is why men and women so often inflict harm on each other instead of bringing the blessing that God created them to enjoy.

> Sin twists commitment into selfishness, intimacy into secrecy and shame, and interdependence into conflict.

Cursed!

The Bible is the message of a gracious, saving God. From this point forward, from the third chapter of Genesis to the last chapter of Revelation, the Bible unfolds God's saving plan to restore sinful mankind and reclaim his paradise lost. And how does this all begin? Surprisingly to us, God begins by uttering three curses upon each of the three participants of the fall into sin: the serpent, the woman, and finally the man. As we will see, these curses are not merely punitive, but ultimately redemptive.

First came the curses on the serpent:

> The LORD God said to the serpent, "Because you have done this, cursed are you above all livestock and above all beasts of the field; on your belly you shall go, and dust you shall eat all the days of your life. I will put enmity between you and the woman, and between your offspring and her offspring; he shall bruise your head, and you shall bruise his heel." (Gen. 3:14–15)

Every Christian should look upon this as a great promise of God's grace. God promises hostility between the devil and his offspring and the woman and her offspring. This describes those who would follow in the ways of the devil and those who would follow Eve in faith. Most especially, God points to a single offspring to come, none other than the Lord Jesus Christ. Him especially the devil would oppose, even to the point of the cross. The serpent "shall bruise his heel," but the Savior son of Eve "shall bruise your head." Here we receive the first preaching of the gospel—the promise of a salvation that comes into the world from God through the saving work of Jesus Christ.

Next came the curse on the woman. To her, God said, "I will surely multiply your pain in childbearing; in pain you shall bring forth children. Your desire shall be for your husband, and he shall rule over you" (Gen. 3:16). Women often focus on the promised pains of childbirth, but more relevant to our discussion is the effect on their relationships with men. God said, "Your desire shall be for your husband, and he shall rule over you." At the heart of this statement is a curse that she will *desire* her husband.

The Hebrew word for *desire* refers to a stretching out for, a running after, or a yearning for. Two other occurrences in the Old Testament help us to understand its range of meaning. The word occurs in the next chapter, in the story of Cain. Cain had committed murder against his brother, Abel, and God warned him that "sin is crouching at the door. Its desire is for you, but you must rule over it" (Gen. 4:7). "Its *desire* is for you" employs the same word that God uses for the way in which the woman will now desire to possess or control the man. Another occurrence is in Song of Solomon 7:10: "I am my beloved's, and his desire is for me." Here, the word is used to convey romantic infatuation.

God's curse on the woman is alive and well today. Go to any checkout counter and look at the contents of so many women's magazines. Page after page, article after article, is devoted to the very things God cursed Eve with:

an obsession with possessing and captivating men, mainly through beauty and sex. If it is true that women tend both to long for a man and to try to control the man they have, the origin of this problem is found in God's curse on Eve.

> God's curse on the woman is alive and
> well. Go to any checkout counter and look
> at the contents of women's magazines—
> an obsession with possessing
> and captivating men.

Given all we have said about God's design in the love relationship, it can hardly be wrong for a woman to desire a man. But God cursed what was good and wholesome so that now it becomes a burden. Eve has turned away from God and put Adam in God's place, so what was meant to be a blessing is now an obsession and inward craving.

We can observe three characteristics of this now-cursed desire of the woman for the man. First, the woman's desire serves her own ends rather than serving first the glory of God and then the well-being of the man. Second, her desire weakens and disarms the man rather than complementing and helping him. Third, her desire for the man is driven by carnal emotions—fear, jealousy, self-pity, anger, pride—rather than by trust in God's design.

The effects of all this are vividly felt both in dating and in marriage. Instead of waiting on God to provide for their need of a companion, women are tempted to manipulate a man into a dating relationship and once they are dating to capture him for marriage. Instead of finding satisfaction first in God, they seek happiness in a man; "their desire is for him," and their attention is fixed on gaining him.

> Instead of waiting on God, women are tempted to manipulate a man and capture him for marriage. Instead of finding satisfaction in God, they seek happiness in a man.

If you are a woman, take a moment to complete these two sentences. "As the deer pants for water, so my soul pants for . . ." (Ps. 43:1). For what? How about this one: "I would be happy if only . . ." If only what? If you complete either of these sentences by using a man's name or referring to a man in general, then you are experiencing the effects of the curse of sin. The woman was made to be a helper to the man, but not to be his worshiper. For you to seek your ultimate fulfillment in a relationship with a man is to be guilty of idolatry. God is your first husband. Only by making God your first love can you put your desire for a man into proper perspective. Remember the essence of the sin into which Adam and Eve fell: it was to deny God's goodness and faithfulness, and to make a god of each other in the place of the one true God. God will not allow anything to rob him of his position and glory in our lives. He will not idly sit by while we worship the gift instead of the Giver, so God placed this curse on the woman. Without God at the center of her life, she finds love with a man to be as much of a burden as a blessing.

Under God's curse, the woman desires not only to have the man but to control him. The second way to understand this curse of desire is in the context of rule. Adam was created to rule: to exercise dominion over the creation and to be the head of the woman (see 1 Cor. 11:3). But now the woman will strive against male rule and manipulate to gain control. Here we have the battle of the sexes, one of the first results of the fall into sin. No doubt Eve has a harder time trusting Adam now that he has shown himself to be a sinner. But, said God to the woman, you will strive against his rule, "and he shall rule over you" (Gen. 3:16). Because of this curse, feminine sin involves disrespect toward men, challenging for control, belittling comments, incessant nagging, and exploiting his weaknesses, all in the place of godly respect and helpful companionship. The man must strive against her for headship, for respect, and for the rule that God gave him over the relationship. "He will rule over you if he can," God is saying, "and you aren't going to like it very much!"

This, too, finds regular expression in our popular culture. Not long ago we passed an interstate billboard that was as obnoxious as it was realistic. Picture this if you can: There is a pitiful-looking guy with his eyes bulging out, his hair standing on end. Behind him is a big, bad woman whose arms are outstretched and ready to pounce on him. It was an advertisement for a new television sitcom, and the caption read, "Behind every good man is a woman kicking his butt." From a woman's perspective, we're to infer, a good man is one controlled by and in fear of a woman. The sad truth is how strongly this dynamic plays out in so many relationships. Men cry out, "She's trying to control me!" and how often it is true. This is God's curse on Eve and thus on the relationship of the man and woman.

Things are looking bad, and we haven't yet even considered the final curse, God's curse on Adam. God saved the man for last, not merely because he was the last to partake of the forbidden fruit, but because God's curses ultimately culminate on him as covenant head.

> To Adam he said, "Because you listened to your wife and ate from the tree about which I commanded you, 'You must not eat of it,' cursed is the ground because of you; through painful toil you will eat of it all the days of your life. It will produce thorns and thistles for you, and you will eat the plants of the field. By the sweat of your brow you will eat your food until you return to the ground, since from it you were taken; for dust you are and to dust you will return." (Gen. 3:17–19, NIV)

So much could be said about this that in the context of our study we can barely scratch the surface. Because of Adam's sin, the whole creation fell into corruption. Adam was commissioned to "work [the Garden] and take care of it" (Gen. 2:15, NIV). But now the earth itself partakes of his condemnation. "Cursed is the ground," God says, because the ground is joined to Adam. The same is true of Adam's labor: "Through painful toil you will eat of it all the days of your life." Childbirth would cause Eve anguish for a few hours at the end of her pregnancies, but Adam's "painful toil" would be a daily occurrence. And at the end of it all, death awaited: "By the sweat of your brow you will eat your food until you return to the ground, since from it you were taken; for dust you are and to dust you will return." Instead of a blessing granted by God, work now becomes a cursed burden for Adam. Instead of enjoying the pleasures of home in contented abundance, he will spend himself in the fields until his own body descends into the dust of death. Just as God cursed the woman's inward focus that was part of his original design, now he curses the man's outward focus. The woman was made to help the man; in sin she seeks to control him. The man was made to lead the relationship as they bore fruit and multiplied; in sin Adam now ignores her under the crushing weight of his own work.

> The man's outward focus is cursed.
> Made to lead the relationship, in sin
> Adam now ignores the woman under
> the crushing weight of his work.

"Why would God do this?" you may ask. If God loved Adam and Eve, why didn't he just forgive them and restore them to blessing? Because God's gifts cannot be enjoyed without obedience to him as the Giver. In sin, Adam and Eve would seek to find love with each other in the absence of love for God, and in God's creation this simply cannot work. To reject God is to fall into sin; to fall into sin is to fall prey to guilt and the power of its corruption, both of which make love impossible as God designed it. It was thus in mercy that God cursed the woman and the man, injecting a poison into their relationship for which he alone is the antidote. In the futility of love apart from God, Adam and Eve were to turn back to God, just as we must turn to God today for grace to repent of sin and minister in love. Love between a man and a woman simply cannot work without love for God at the center of the relationship; by means of his curses, God mercifully brings this fact to our attention so as to woo us back to himself.

> Love between a man and a woman
> simply cannot work without love for God
> at the center of the relationship.

East of Eden

Genesis 3 ends ominously. We read in verses 23–24 (NIV), "The LORD God banished him from the Garden of Eden to work the ground from which he had been taken. After he drove the man out, he placed on the east side of the Garden of Eden cherubim and a flaming sword flashing back and forth to guard the way to the tree of life." This is where human history thus takes place, because of sin. This is where we live, in the thorn-cursed world where everything is hard, nothing more so than the relationship between a man and a woman. But there is hope even here. The verses preceding this conclusion tell us of how Adam and Eve turned to God in faith and in return received the promise of salvation. Verse 20 (NIV) says, "Adam named his wife Eve, because she would become the mother of all the living." Adam had accepted God's promise of an offspring who would come through the womb of his wife. Finally, after all this time, he has found the right name for her; it is only here that the name Eve is given her by Adam. It means *mother*, and by it Adam expressed their joint faith in the salvation that God had promised.

We know this because of what God did in response: "The LORD God made garments of skin for Adam and his wife and clothed them" (Gen. 3:21, NIV). God clothed them with the innocent garment of a sacrificial offering. Ultimately this pointed forward to the righteousness that comes through faith in Jesus Christ, the woman's seed, who brings salvation to the sinful race. By this means, God restored the man and the woman to himself. In fellowship with him the curse could be redeemed, love as God intended could be regained, and even East of Eden, God's blessing could be restored to the man and woman together. It is to this, the redemption of the relationship, that we now turn.

> By the sacrifice of Christ, the curse can be redeemed, love can be regained, and God's blessing can be restored.

3

"Put on Love"

The Relationship Redeemed in Christ

WHEN IT COMES TO LOVE, many people are so discouraged that they are ready to throw in the towel. That is true of many couples in marriage, and it is true of many singles hoping for marriage. So far, our tour of the Bible has offered little encouragement. If the problem is this bad, who can fix it? The answer is that God can fix the problem of our sin, and he does so through the redeeming work of our Savior, Jesus Christ. This is the glory of Christianity: that we are saved not just from our sin but also to the blessings for which God first created us and now has redeemed us through the blood of his only Son. This means that we *can* share and enjoy blessings together as man and woman.

Here is good news for those who have struggled in dating relationships, and especially for a Christian couple seeking instruction from the Lord. In the next two chapters, we will examine the Bible's teaching on love. Some of it comes from passages that pertain directly to marriage, from which we can derive principles that will inform a serious dating relationship. Other passages deal more generally with how Christians should treat one another. The Bible provides solid teaching on how to love. But God gives us more than good advice; he redeems us so that we have the power to love as he designed. His love is so great that it enables us to love even in the same way that Christ loved the church. This is the good news of our redemption in Christ.

> God does more than give us good advice.
> He redeems us so that we have
> the power to love as he designed.

God First!

The greatest problem of our lives is that we are alienated from God and out of step with his ways. This is the core issue of sin; everything else is a symptom of this crucial problem. Therefore, redemption starts by restoring us to our relationship with God. This is how Genesis 3 ended and why there was hope for our first parents. God promised a Savior. When Adam and Eve trusted his Word, God previewed for them the saving work of Jesus Christ. He slew an innocent animal in their place and clothed them in its skin to cover their sin. This pointed forward to Jesus' death on the cross for our sins; when we trust in Jesus, our sins are forgiven and we are clothed in his perfect righteousness before God. Instead of hiding from God and covering our sins with the fig leaves of good works or mere outward religion, God himself provides us with a spotless robe purchased with the blood of Christ.

This is where a redeemed love relationship begins between a man and a woman. The problems arose from sin, and the solutions flow from God's remedy for sin. It is only as a man and woman come in faith before the cross of Jesus and find themselves restored to God that their own relationship can be redeemed from the guilt and the power of sin. We find the ability to love one another rather than using one another to meet our needs and desires.

Only at the cross of Christ can a relationship be redeemed from the guilt and the power of sin.

This alone should make it abundantly clear that a Christian has no business dating someone who has not come to faith in Christ. A relationship between a Christian and an unbeliever is powerless to enjoy the blessings of Christ's redeeming work, for the simple reason that it is based on unbelief and rebellion rather than faith in God's Word. Second Corinthians 6:14–15 warns, "Do not be unequally yoked with unbelievers. For what partnership has righteousness with lawlessness? Or what fellowship has light with darkness? What accord has Christ with Belial? Or what portion does a believer share with an unbeliever?" This, like all of God's other commands, is not a cruel barrier to our happiness, but a loving restriction that preserves us for God's blessing. The blessings that we are hoping for come from God alone. Therefore, we must start with obedience to his Word. Only a relationship in which both partners are Christians can possibly result in the kind of love that only God can give.

A redeemed relationship begins with the man and the woman individually coming to God and turning to him as the Lord and Savior of their lives. Whereas sin sought to dethrone God, redemption submits to him and seeks his glory in all things. Turning to God means that we ultimately seek our satisfaction in him, and that we acknowledge and completely trust him to fulfill us, apart from anything or anyone else. It means making God our God, and repenting of all the idols that previously dominated our lives.

Psalm 16 is a wonderful portion of Scripture, especially for Christians struggling to find all their satisfaction in God. This is essential if we are to have healthy love relationships, for only when we are finding our ultimate satisfaction in God are we able to relate rightly to one another. Let's take some time to work through the psalm together, as Israel's King David leads us along a path that begins with faith and leads to the joy of the Lord.

Psalm 16 begins with a great statement of faith, in verses 1–2: "Preserve me, O God, for in you I take refuge. I say to the LORD, 'You are my Lord; I have no good apart from you.'" This is what it means to entrust ourselves to God; we take our refuge in him and acknowledge that he alone can provide the blessings we desire. It also means that though we possess everything we desire, without God we will never be satisfied.

David then applies this statement of faith to his actual circumstances, using it as a lens to gain a right perspective on his life: "As for the saints in the land, they are the excellent ones, in whom is all my delight. The sorrows of those who run after another god shall multiply; their drink offerings of blood I will not pour out or take their names on my lips" (vv. 3–4). Instead of envying what others seem to have, he discerns the end result of a godless life. He resolves not to follow in their ways but to commit himself wholly to the Lord. Others may look happy, but without God their hearts will never be at rest; yet the believer can always rest his or her heart in the hands of God.

Knowing that he or she can trust in God, and confident that God will provide for all the needs of life, the godly man or woman submits to God's provision and praises God for the wisdom with which he is overseeing his or her life: "The Lord is my chosen portion and my cup; you hold my lot. The lines have fallen for me in pleasant places; indeed, I have a beautiful inheritance" (vv. 5 6). The believer knows that whatever he has or lacks is from the Lord; he delights to know that it is a good and wise God who portions his blessings, the greatest of which is himself. If the believer has God, that is more than enough.

Psalm 16:1–6 takes us down a path that starts with faith and leads through discernment into submission to God's will as it is working out in our lives. Have you taken this path that alone can enable you to find your blessings in the Lord? These verses contain the secret to Christian joy and fulfillment: what follows in the psalm shows God's blessings on his faithful, submissive child.

Verses 7–8 contain the first of these blessings, which is an ability to worship the Lord always. David writes, "I bless the Lord who gives me counsel; in the night also my heart instructs me. I have set the Lord always before me; because he is at my right hand, I shall not be shaken" (vv. 7–8). What a blessing that is, because we were made to worship God. Worship leads to the next blessing, which is joy in the Lord: "Therefore my heart is glad, and my whole being rejoices; my flesh also dwells secure. For you will not abandon my soul to Sheol, or let your holy one see corruption" (vv. 9–10). Joy comes through a life of worship, and rest in the Lord leads to the kind of fulfillment that David expresses in the psalm's closing verse: "You make known to me the path of life; in your presence there is fullness of joy; at your right hand are pleasures forevermore" (v. 11).

> Joy comes through a life of worship: "You make known to me the path of life; in your presence there is fullness of joy . . ." (Ps. 16:11).

The point of Psalm 16 is the great lesson that all of us need to learn; it is a course of instruction that we will spend the rest of our lives trying to master. It teaches us the first lesson for our relationships, namely, that God is the one we are to worship and that by worshiping him we find true joy and the satisfaction that our souls long for. What liberty this gives us to really love another person! If God is my portion, if God is the true source of my joy, and if it is God who will fulfill me, then I am free to be a companion instead of a consumer. That is, because of what I receive from God I can give to another person instead of always taking; I can minister rather than manipulate because of the fulfillment I get from God.

From Manipulation to Ministry

How much our relationships change when we no longer seek to make a god of one another! Putting God first entirely changes the way we relate to others. Under sin, we treat each other one way; under redemption, we find a different way of love.

Consider what an idolatrous relationship looks like, one that is under the power of sin, in which God's place is taken by another person or power. We are all worshipers, and whatever we worship we rely upon and serve. For many men, success is the god they worship and serve. For others, it is fame or pleasure. Women often worship beauty or falling in love. Whatever it is, we worship it because we think it will make our lives work. It will secure us against a hostile world, it will give us satisfaction—in short, it will be our Savior. Thus, when an idolater says, "I love you," what he means is, "You are a means for getting what I want. You are serving my needs and securing my hopes."

How, then, under the power of their idols, do a man and woman relate to each other? The answer is *manipulation*. Using a variety of tactics, the man manipulates the woman to get what he wants and to serve the gods that he worships. The woman, serving her own gods, manipulates him in return. If compatibility exists between their mutual idol-worship, then each is willing to meet the demands of the other's idols. In this situation, there may be a minimum of conflict, although there will also be little of the intimacy that God intended for their relationship. But if their respective idol-worship is not compatible, as is usually the case, conflict and misery are certain to ensue. Each wants something that the other can give or that the other can help him or her achieve, be it riches, fame, success, pleasure, or just personal peace. But the other has things he or she wants, idols he or she serves, and the pursuit of these things governs his or her heart as well. Needing to get something from the other in order to be content, the couple is caught in the grips of a relationship based on mutual manipulation.

Manipulation: "You are a means
for me to get what I want."

Often, a man and woman are initially motivated to please each other; this is especially common early in a dating relationship. If the man is an egotist, the woman learns to compliment him. If the woman is possessed by worldly ambition, the man tries to exhibit competence. Their idols are nicely fed and served, so things move forward. But as the relationship matures, they each begin to see their partner's idols for what they are and to realize that they are not going away. The man's idols begin to shape his attitude about the woman: she resents his long hours at work, she is not beautiful enough, she demands time and attention that he does not want to give. The woman's idols also speak out—he is not confident enough, he doesn't pay enough attention, her friends aren't as impressed as she thought they would be. This is what we often mean when we say that we have fallen out of love. When first dating, the feeling of our needs being met was mistaken for love; now that they are no longer being met, we find that the loving feeling is also gone. Such self-centered love promotes manipulation, and when manipulation fails, the end of love has arrived.

An idolater has an implicit contract with his idol. A man who worships success has agreed to work extraordinary hours, or to do more than all his peers, or to internalize every company value and goal. A woman whose identity requires a great deal of attention will come into conflict with such a man. At first, she may be proud to be seen with him, and he may be drawn by her admiration. But their conflicting idol-contracts demand a reckoning, and the result is conflict, to which each responds by manipulating the other in order to serve his or her god.

When it comes to manipulation, we can use any number of strategies. For instance, a man who worships pleasure may cajole his girlfriend into illicit sex by being attentive, or perhaps critical; he may threaten the relationship or write a poem that he thinks will stir up romance in her heart. What he wants is not a committed relationship but pleasure, so he holds out the bait of possible commitment as a means to his desired end. The actual tactic does not matter much; the point is that he is manipulating her to get what he wants. That is the way idolatrous love works.

But let's not forget the woman. Perhaps she thinks it is marriage that will make her happy; by worshiping the false god of possessing a man, she expects to be blessed. So she, too, manipulates. Perhaps she offers him sexual pleasure, or perhaps she withholds it; she may complain, or perhaps play to his ego. However the game is actually played, the strategy is one of manipulation. The goal is to get the man to place the idol of her desire into her hands.

These are just examples. Different people have different idols. As we saw in the curses of Genesis 3, the woman's idols will often be relationship-oriented; she desires to possess *him* as the key to her happiness. But there are differences among women; some want a luxurious lifestyle, some want prestige and excitement, others want a quiet home in the country. Similarly, Genesis 3 told us that men will often be motivated by idols external to the relationship: money, power, excitement. Whatever they are, the point is that idols must be served, and the dating or marriage partner must be coerced into contributing to that service. This, by the way, is often what the world means by "compatibility." The key to a happy relationship, the experts tell us, is to find a companion who worships the same idols that you do, or whose idols are at least not in conflict with your own. This is a fool's paradise, for sin and idolatry never truly produce harmony but always strife.

It is because of idolatry that most relationships are marred by conflict. The problem in our relationships—and sadly, this includes Christians—is that our sinful idolatries are in conflict. This is what James describes in James 4:1–2: "What causes quarrels and what causes fights among you? Is it not this, that your passions are at war within you? You desire and do not have, so you murder. You covet and cannot obtain, so you fight and quarrel." What is more, since idols never satisfy, but always demand more and more, conflict is inevitable and progressively gets worse. Idols never satisfy, but always demand increasingly more, constantly adding to the burdens of our lives and in the end giving nothing of lasting value.

> Idols never satisfy, but always demand increasingly more, adding to the burden of our lives while giving nothing of lasting value.

A relationship based on idolatry can result only in manipulation and conflict. But how different it is when a man and woman come together in worship of the one true God! Here is a compatibility based neither on shared idolatrous interests (an unstable foundation if ever there was one) nor on a pursuit of false gods that can never really satisfy. It is a union that trusts in the God who gives instead of takes, who saves and blesses his people. Jesus said, "The Son of Man came not to be served but to serve" (Matt. 20:28). The true God is one who fulfills the desires of our hearts, who, as David said in Psalm 16, fills us with joy in his presence. This is what God said to Israel, contrasting himself with the burdensome idols of Babylon: "Even to your old age and gray hairs I am he, I am he who will sustain you. I have made you and I will carry you; I will sustain you and I will rescue you" (Isa. 46:4, NIV).

The distinction between the false gods and the one true God makes all the difference in our lives and relationships. Because God meets the needs of those who trust in him, a Christian relationship is one that escapes the cycle of manipulation. In the place of manipulation there is *ministry*. This is the approach of Christians who are finding their fulfillment in the Lord as they relate to one another. Having their needs met by God, they enjoy a relationship of service to one another. This is the dynamic that distinguishes a healthy, godly relationship from a worldly, idolatrous one. Manipulation gives way to ministry, in fulfillment of God's two great commands to love God and to love our neighbor as ourselves.

> Manipulation gives way to ministry:
> a relationship of serving one another
> in fulfillment of God's two great commands.

"Putting on" Love

How are we to think about ministering to one another in love? One of the best-loved passages in the Bible that teaches this is Colossians 3:12–17. This passage adorned the bulletin for our own wedding service, as it has for so many others, and it has been a helpful guide in turning from the manipulation in which we are all so steeped to the ministry that God desires. In beautiful language, the apostle Paul writes:

> Put on then, as God's chosen ones, holy and beloved, compassion, kindness, humility, meekness, and patience, bearing with one another and, if one has a complaint against another, forgiving each other; as the Lord has forgiven you, so you also must forgive. And above all these put on love, which binds everything together in perfect harmony. And let the peace of Christ rule in your hearts, to which indeed you were called in one body. And be thankful. Let the word of Christ dwell in you richly, teaching and admonishing one another in all wisdom, singing psalms and hymns and spiritual songs, with thankfulness in your hearts to God. And whatever you do, in word or deed, do everything in the name of the Lord Jesus, giving thanks to God the Father through him.

What Paul describes here are the *resources* of God's grace and our *response* in relationship to others. First is God's work for us. God chose us to be his people. As Paul wrote in Ephesians 1:4, "He chose us in [Christ] before the foundation of the world." We did not become God's people because of our own goodness or greatness, but by God's gracious election. Furthermore, because of God's grace, we are holy to him and beloved to his heart. Colossians 3:13 reminds us that if we are Christians, God has forgiven our sins because of Christ's death on the cross. Added to God's work *for* us is God's work *in* us. In verse 15, Paul speaks of "the peace of Christ" within us, a peace that tells us that our future is secure and that our present is filled with God's loving purpose. When Christ's peace rules in our hearts, as Paul exhorts us, then we are no longer governed by selfish motives or by anger or envy or resentment. This particularly finds expression through the grace of thanksgiving. God's work in our lives makes us grateful for the many blessings we enjoy. Finally, Paul says in verse 16, "Let the word of Christ dwell in you richly." These resources combine to enable us to love as he has loved us: the peace of Christ, the grace of thanksgiving, and God's living and active Word.

If we want to learn to love, then this is the way: by letting Christ rule our hearts, with thanksgiving, as his Word dwells richly in us, teaching and admonishing us in the way of God's love. These are the resources of God's grace, and apart from them we will find it beyond our ability to experience and to share the love we long for in our relationships.

> The resources of God's grace: God's work for us—his electing love and Christ's atoning blood—and God's work *in us*—the peace of Christ ruling our hearts.

The apostle John says that we love because God first loved us (1 John 4:19). It is out of these resources that we are to respond in grace to one another. Paul presents this response to God's love for us in two steps. First, we allow his grace to shape our lives: "Put on then, as God's chosen ones, holy and beloved, compassion, kindness, humility, meekness, and patience" (Col. 3:12). This means that if

65

you are hoping to become the kind of person who can succeed in a love relationship, you must start by cultivating these virtues. Or, if you are in a relationship and are seeking for it to grow in a healthy way, you need to focus on these things. This is the way to love: to respond to God's grace for you by showing compassion, by acting kindly, through a humble and meek and patient demeanor.

Paul's second step is to especially employ these virtues when friction or sin enters into the relationship, when you are let down or bothered by each other: "bearing with one another and, if one has a complaint against another, forgiving each other; as the Lord has forgiven you, so you also must forgive" (v. 13). Is it hard to forgive when you have been hurt? Yes, it is. But it is impossible to grow in a healthy relationship unless sin can be conquered by repentance and by loving forgiveness. If we are to love, we must be able to humble ourselves in repentance when we have done wrong and to forgive when our partner has done wrong, both of which are made possible only by our awareness of God's forgiveness in Jesus Christ.

Paul concludes, "And above all these put on love, which binds everything together in perfect harmony" (v. 14). A romantic relationship begins with attraction and then grows through affection for each other. But a relationship matures toward true and godly love as it ripens into a desire to give, a longing to bless, and a willingness to sacrifice and to serve. The Bible gives the highest expression of love in terms of God's gift of his only Son, Jesus Christ: "For God so loved the world, that he gave his only Son" (John 3:16). This is the love with which we are to bind our thoughts and words, our feelings and interactions. The result, when two people love with the love that comes from God, is that most wonderful realization of unity, in which two people give all of their individuality into what Paul calls a "perfect harmony."

Christian love involves our response to God's grace: putting on godly virtues, bearing with and forgiving one another, and offering the sacrificial love we have received from Jesus Christ.

4

God's Blueprint for Love

The Relationship Redeemed in Christ, Part 2

ONCE WE GOT TO COLLEGE, we finally understood high school. We know what it is like to start our first jobs, fresh out of college, eager to succeed. We know the joys and particular pitfalls. Similarly, we think we understand dating now that we are married. Perhaps years from now we will understand parenting a little better than we do now; with five little children, we're feeling pretty rough around the edges. Is it our fate to understand life's challenges only once we are past them, only when we no longer really need such knowledge?

Writing as a married couple, we have come to realize, gratefully, that the answer is "No." We are not consigned to ignorance of things while we are going through them, only to gain objectivity once we are past these particular challenges. It is true that in the heart of a struggle it is next to impossible for us to be objective and clear-headed on our own. Fortunately, we have found that there is one source of objective, surefooted counsel even for the challenges we feel right now pressing on our hearts. That source of wisdom and truth is none other than God's inerrant and authoritative Word, the operators' manual written by our Creator himself.

The material we will present in this chapter will revolutionize any relationship that is floundering and will establish a new relationship on a sure and godly foundation. That is quite a claim! But it is God's own blueprint for love between a man and a woman, requiring us merely to trust and obey him. It is simple, but certainly not easy. It takes the building blocks of a man and a woman each committed to God through faith in Jesus Christ, the plain teaching of God's Word for their manner of relating to each other, and the active involvement of God himself, who delights to reward his obedient children with the blessings of love. In other words, it is a miracle of grace, that is, the ordinary kind of miracle that happens when two Christian people, one a man and the other a woman, commit themselves to the covenant of love that God sets before them in the Bible.

The Redeemed Man

So far, we have considered general principles for a redeemed relationship. It is impossible to overestimate the importance of turning to God for salvation and then ministering to each other out of the resources of his grace. But just as the pattern of sin and God's curse took on one particular form for the woman and another for the man, so too does redemption involve a particular response from the Christian woman and the Christian man.

Here is another occasion when we will rely on the Bible's teaching regarding marriage to inform our views of godly dating. The New Testament offers two extended passages on marriage, one in Ephesians 5:22–33 and the other in 1 Peter 3:1–7. The two passages fit together, although they contain slightly different emphases. By acting according to the pattern set forth in them, the Christian man and woman may progress in their dating relationship in a way that is fitted for what God has ordained for their blessing in marriage.

Let's first consider Paul's teaching on marriage in Ephesians 5:22–28. The first thing this passage says to the man is that God expects him to lead the redeemed relationship: "The husband is the head of the wife even as Christ is the head of the church" (Eph. 5:23). Adam was established as lord of the Garden, with Eve as his helper and companion. So it is to be in marriage. In a dating relationship, a man does not have a right to expect submission from the woman, since this obligation is reserved for marriage. But backtracking this principle into a dating relationship, a man should take it as his responsibility to lead the relationship, ensuring that it honors God and is a blessing to the woman he is dating.

A Christian man should take responsibility for the dating relationship, ensuring that it honors God and blesses the woman.

A Christian man should seek to win the respect of the woman he is dating. His outlook is shaped by a husband's duty to love his wife: "Husbands, love your wives, as Christ loved the church and gave himself up for her" (v. 25). This does not require a man to fall in love on the first date. But if he is to love a woman, it is to be the kind of self-sacrificing love shown to us by the Lord Jesus Christ. Jesus "gave himself up" for his bride, the church, dying on the cross for our sins. Likewise, the Christian man is to put the spiritual and emotional well-being of a woman he is dating ahead of his own needs and desires. Unlike the norm for worldly men, the Christian is not to exploit the woman sexually, emotionally, or otherwise, but to minister to her needs so that she will be blessed.

Many men think of the call to give themselves for a woman solely in terms of her protection. They say, "I would defend her if there was trouble. If someone attacked her, I would step up for her protection." But they fail to realize that when a woman enters a dating relationship, she mainly needs to be protected from the sins of the very man to whom she is offering her heart. The enemy that men need to stand up to is the one who lives within themselves: the one who is selfish, insensitive, and uncommitted. It is when that man is put to death that the woman will be safe and will be blessed in the relationship.

> The enemy that men need to stand up to is the one who lives within themselves: the one who is selfish, insensitive, and uncommitted.

Paul reminds us that Christ's goal in dying for his bride was "that he might sanctify her" (v. 26). This, too, must be the Christian man's concern for the woman he is with. He determines that whatever happens in the relationship, she will have been spiritually built up. It is largely through his speech that the man has this influence on a woman. Paul continues: "having cleansed her by the washing of water with the word" (v. 26). It is through the Word that Jesus seeks to "present the church to himself in splendor, without spot or wrinkle or any such thing, that she might be holy and without blemish" (v. 27). Through his words (and works), especially as they minister the gospel, a man is to tend the spiritual beauty and well-being of a woman, presenting her to Christ without wrinkle or spot, pure in heart and radiant in faith.

Paul concludes, "In the same way husbands should love their wives as their own bodies. He who loves his wife loves himself" (vv. 28–29). Just as God placed Adam in the Garden of Eden "to work it and keep it" (Gen. 2:15)—those words might equally be translated "to nurture and to protect it"—God also places a man in a relationship with a woman so that she will grow spiritually within the safe confines of his loving care. This is masculine love, as defined by God: to nurture and to protect. Men are to show a protective and nurturing concern for women that equals (or surpasses) their instinctive concern for their own bodies. As Christian men do this, the women in their lives will shine with the spiritual beauty that is precious to God.

The second main New Testament passage that deals with marriage is found in 1 Peter 3:1–7. Here the bulk of the exposition applies to the woman, leaving just one verse to deal with the man. But what an instructive verse it is! Peter says, "Husbands, live with your wives in an understanding way, showing honor to the woman as the weaker vessel, since they are heirs with you of the grace of life, so that your prayers may not be hindered" (v. 7).

A more literal translation would begin, "Live with your wives according to knowledge." This means that husbands are to pay attention to their wives: to get to know them, to notice their vulnerabilities, to become aware of what cares and anxieties are burdening their hearts, and then to make those cares their own. A husband is to minister to his wife, helping her to bear sadness and burdens and also sharing her hopes and joys.

How does this translate into a dating relationship? Quite easily. This is the kind of intimacy that a man and woman should develop while dating (rather than an intimacy based on sex). A godly man will seek to become knowledgeable about the woman he is spending time with and not just about how she looks and what kind of fun she likes to have. A healthy dating relationship is one in which the marital ideal is progressively taking place. It is where the woman can entrust her heart to the man and be blessed by his caring ministry of encouragement and help.

> A godly man will seek to know the woman
> he is dating—not just how she looks and
> what kind of fun she likes to have. She should
> be able to entrust her heart to his ministry
> of encouragement.

The second action in this verse is "showing honor." A godly man looks upon his wife, or the woman he is dating, as much more than a means to his own ends. She is not there just to give him pleasure, either physically or emotionally. He is to ascribe value to her as a person and to see her as a fitting recipient of his ministry. When Paul speaks of a woman as the "weaker vessel," he does not demean her in any way. The fact is that women are in a position of vulnerability with respect to men. They are generally more emotionally vulnerable because God has created them with feminine tenderness. Furthermore, in her obedience to God a Christian wife places herself into the hands of her husband. She becomes dependent on him, especially when she bears his children. Instead of resenting the care that must be taken with a woman's heart, a Christian man should value her all the more. Her vulnerability is part of her beauty; she is of great value to him precisely because God has fitted her to bring out the best in his godly masculinity.

That, says Peter, is what a man is to do with respect to a woman: he is to pay attention as he lives with his wife, becoming aware of what is going on in her heart and ministering to foster her well-being. As he does so, he is to act and speak in a way that conveys the dignity and the value he places on her. Instead of belittling a woman's emotional concerns and begrudging the ministry this calls for, a godly man will express the worth of her heart and the value he places on the ministry that she needs from him. He should be eager to sacrifice for her well-being. This is the pattern that God has set for marriage, and a godly man will begin to practice it during a dating relationship. When he does, the result will be a woman who blossoms and whose love for him grows proportionately to his care.

Peter then adds two perspectives that men are to realize. The first is that wives "are heirs with you of the grace of life." Remember what we observed back in the Garden. When God made mankind in his own image, he did so by creating them "male" and "female" (Gen. 1:27). A woman's heart bears God's image differently than a man's does, but no less accurately. Indeed, with only the masculine qualities that men exhibit, God's image is not completely displayed in this world. Men must realize that those feminine qualities that seem so baffling (and to a certain extent always will) are things of beauty and honor that manifest aspects of the image of God. Far from wishing that a woman's perspective could just be ignored or somehow fixed, Christian men should look upon women with wonder and joy—indeed, with the very delight once expressed by Adam in the Garden!

Furthermore, God warns men that, given their authoritative position over women, they should not take lightly the responsibility that goes with it. Peter reminds men not to neglect the care of women, "so that your prayers may not be hindered." This recalls the prophet Malachi, who rebuked the men of Jerusalem in his day for their treatment of their wives. They wondered why the Lord "no longer regards the offering or accepts it with favor from your hand," that is, why God did not receive their worship or answer their prayers. The reason, said the prophet, was their unfaithfulness to their wives: "Because the LORD was witness between you and the wife of your youth, to whom you have been faithless, though she is your companion and your wife by covenant" (Mal. 2:13–14). Malachi's point was that the wives whom the Israelite men were neglecting, and in some cases discarding, were precious to the Lord. So it is for Christian women placed in the hands of Christian men. God values them with a great love, and men who think their treatment of a Christian woman's heart will not affect their own relationship with God are seriously mistaken. She is Daddy's little girl!

A Christian woman bears God's image differently from a man, but no less. God values her with great love, and his relationship with a man is affected by the man's treatment of Daddy's little girl!

Here are some specific suggestions for how a Christian man can put these principles into action in a dating relationship:

1. Commit to take the lead in the godliness of your relationship. Read the Bible's passages about how men and women and all Christians should treat one another. Especially take the lead in establishing boundaries that will keep you from sexual sin. Assume that this woman is going to be your wife or the wife of some other Christian brother (who might be currently dating your future wife). Treat her as the precious sister in Christ that she is.

2. Decide in advance whether or not you are willing to love a woman in the self-sacrificing, nurturing way the Bible describes. Until you are ready to faithfully hold a woman's heart in your hand, do not enter into a dating relationship.

3. Realizing that God wants you to learn to put her interests ahead of your own, ask her the kinds of things she likes to do and be eager to spend time doing them.

4. Be willing to talk about the relationship. Initiate honest dialogue about how you feel. Do not resent her desire to have the relationship defined, but protect her heart by making your level of commitment clear and thereby making clear the appropriate kind of intimacy to go along with that commitment.

5. Pay attention to her heart. Ask her about her burdens and cares. Seek ways to minister to her and to make her cares your own. Instead of being critical of her, speak words of encouragement and support.

6. Do not be shy in ministering the Word of God to her. Do not preach, but exhort her and call to mind

God's promises and God's love for her in Jesus
Christ. Make it a primary goal that she will be spiritually stronger by having been in a relationship
with you.

7. If something about her bothers you, think about
    how you can encourage her in that area. Realize
    that none of us is without flaws. Pray for her weak-
    ness and try to strengthen her in that area. If your
    concerns are enough to deter you from wanting to
    marry her, let her know in a forthright manner
    while being as considerate as possible.

The Redeemed Woman

The guys have had their turn, so let's talk about the
ladies. Who is the redeemed woman? How can you recognize her? Like the redeemed man, she is submitted to
God and to his Word. The Lord is her first love and the one
who ultimately provides for her heart. Isaiah 54:5 (NIV)
says of her, "For your Maker is your husband—the LORD
Almighty is his name. . . ."

A redeemed woman is one who has entered into a personal relationship with Jesus Christ through faith. Her sins
are forgiven, and she knows God's love. She fears the Lord,
realizing that blessing for her comes through obedience
to his Word. His commands are not burdensome to her,
and her heart is not set on worldly treasures. She attends
regular worship and approaches her life with prayer. She
enjoys healthy fellowship with other believers and bears
observable fruit in ministry to others. She answers God's
calling in her life while single, not waiting for marriage to
give her happiness or purpose.

What kind of woman is this? The answer: a healthy,
spiritually mature Christian woman—the kind that God

78

can and does make. Our point is not that a redeemed woman has to be perfect. Far from it! But the single Christian woman can and must embrace a life of redemption through faith in Jesus Christ. The very things a woman needs in order to contribute to a healthy love relationship are the things she gains through growth in relationship with Christ. It is gratitude and love for the Lord and his great mercy toward her as an undeserving sinner that fuels her obedience to his Word in marriage and while dating. A woman need not be married to be a redeemed woman, but to enjoy marriage as God designed, she certainly must be redeemed.

Let's remember what we have already learned from the Bible about the redeemed woman. The first thing the Bible says about a woman is that she is made in God's image and that her life is given for his glory. In relationship to a man, she is given as a helper (see ch. 1 and Gen. 2:18). She does not resent this position or feel devalued by God's ordering of creation. This means that in a relationship, she ministers to a man through the role of helper. In dating, she helps the man by letting him lead the relationship and honoring God alongside him. She helps him by being respectful of his ideas and his relationship to the Lord. This does not mean going along with a man even if he wants to lead her into sin! But it does mean that she helps him to conduct their relationship in a God-honoring way.

Christian women sometimes complain that the men they are dating are their spiritual inferiors, or that they cannot respect a man because they "know more" than he does. It is true that a woman is foolish to give her heart to a man who is spiritually uncommitted or is truly immature in his relationship with God. But often a woman can encourage a man who is committed to Christ, even if he is not as far along as she is. She can praise him for what he understands about godliness. She can ask him for spiritual counsel and prayer, and encourage him in his study of God's Word. Instead of belittling him for what he does not know, she can find encouragement in the fruit that he is starting to bear in Christ. The Christian woman may foolishly complain that her man lacks spiritual stature, when it is God's calling for her to help build the man up and to inspire him to that very thing. Moreover, a wise Christian woman realizes that it takes a man time to get to know a woman; she helps him in this effort and minimizes the demands she places upon him, especially early in a relationship.

This word *helper* provides a wealth of counsel to a Christian woman in a dating relationship. Instead of simply demanding and always evaluating a man, she helps him to do and to be those things that God calls for in his life and in their relationship. She helps the relationship honor God by saying "no" when necessary. She treats him as a brother in Christ whom God is making more holy, and not as her own personal savior who must fulfill her every desire.

> The woman ministers to the man in the role of helper. She helps him to do and to be what God calls for. She treats him as a brother in Christ, not as a savior who is to fulfill her every desire.

Moreover, a redeemed woman gives valuable help by her virtue and industry. This is the woman described in Proverbs 31: "A wife of noble character who can find? She is worth far more than rubies. Her husband has full confidence in her and lacks nothing of value. She brings him good, not harm, all the days of her life" (vv. 10–12, NIV). Can you see what is happening here? The redeemed woman is one who operates under the idea of doing good to her husband rather than trying to possess him. He gains confidence in her through her ministry to him. He finds commitment to her attractive and not scary. He can trust her, rather than having to look behind his back to see how she is trying to take advantage of him. They share a purpose, and they are a team.

Men should realize that the women they marry will raise their children, spend their money, manage their home, be trusted with wedding vows, and partner with them in life-changing decisions. It is important that men choose wisely. "Is this woman one who will help me or hinder me?" a godly man wisely inquires. Therefore, women who wish to be chosen by wise men will cultivate virtue and practice industry. A godly man who wishes to choose wisely will keep Proverbs 31:30 (NIV) in mind, and a woman who seeks to attract such a man will take it to heart: "Charm is deceptive, and beauty is fleeting; but a woman who fears the LORD is to be praised."

> Men: The woman you marry will
> raise your children, spend your money,
> manage your home, and partner in your
> life-changing decisions. "A woman
> who fears the LORD is to be praised."

Just as God's Word gives men a blueprint for their relationship with women, so also do Christian women find clear instruction from the Lord. The main passage to which women should refer is Ephesians 5:22–24. Paul writes, "Wives, submit to your own husbands, as to the Lord. For the husband is the head of the wife even as Christ is the head of the church, his body, and is himself its Savior. Now as the church submits to Christ, so also wives should submit in everything to their husbands." Colossians 3:18 adds, "Wives, submit to your husbands, as is fitting in the Lord." Peter takes the same approach, writing in 1 Peter 3:1, "Wives, be subject to your own husbands."

If being called a "helper" outrages some women, "submission" is a word that sends women running right out the door. Undoubtedly, in some instances women have been demeaned and kept quiet in unbiblical ways through a poor understanding of submission. But this does not give women the right to reject God's Word, choosing instead to make their own rules. As Psalm 19:8 asserts, "The precepts of the Lord are right, rejoicing the heart; the commandment of the Lord is pure, enlightening the eyes." The pattern that God gives for men and women in relationship is the one way for sin to be redeemed in love and blessing. In a world of strife, God has provided this way for us to love one another and live in harmony. It is for this reason that Paul commands wives to submit to their husbands "as to the Lord" (Eph. 5:22). "As the church submits to Christ," he says, "so also wives should submit in everything to their husbands" (v. 24).

When we looked at the effects of sin on the relationship and at God's curse on the woman, we noticed how sin produces disorder and conflict. So God gives submission as a blessing so that men and women may work together without hostility or resentment. Wives help their husbands by placing themselves under their authority. It encourages men who have been reluctant to assume a role of leadership to do so, and it helps them to bear the weight of this responsibility. No husband can effectively lead a home without the active and practical assistance of his wife. In the place of resentment, a man feels admiration and love for her, and is encouraged to cherish his wife and to care for her heart. The woman's submission is a reflection of her belief in God's sovereignty, goodness, and wisdom, and shows how her faith has freed her to escape the bonds of fear (see 1 Peter 3:6).

Feminine submission is kinetic. It is active. A wife submits voluntarily, not merely as demanded and enforced by the man. It is a gift that a woman offers to the man she has vowed to love in obedience to the God who first loved her. For this reason, it is imperative that a woman's submission be "as to the Lord," that is, flowing from the submissive obedience she already yields to Jesus Christ. The phrase "for the husband is the head of the wife" (Eph. 5:23) teaches that women submit to husbands because that is the order God established at creation—not because men are superior. Since opposition to any authority is embedded in the curse of sin, a Christian woman's submission can come about only by the Spirit of God, as the fruit that comes from a life in union with Christ. "I am the vine; you are the branches," Jesus said. "Apart from me you can do nothing" (John 15:5). How true that is of submission!

> Feminine submission is kinetic,
> an active gift of worship to Jesus Christ.

The man is not the only one who benefits from the submission of his wife. The benefits to the woman are considerable as well. The headship of a godly man gives protection and provides a healthy environment for the woman's spiritual growth and joy, and she has the peace of knowing that she is living in accordance with God's will. The path of obedience to God's Word is for her the path of God's blessing.

This book is about dating, however, not about marriage. So how does submission apply for the woman in a dating relationship? Much in every way! If the woman is dating with an eye toward marriage, God's command informs her as to the kind of man whom she hopes to attract and whom she should be willing to date. The man need not yet be a spiritual giant; indeed, it will be rare for a man who has yet to experience the benefits of marriage to match up to married role models. But a Christian woman needs to know that the man to whom she is potentially going to submit is himself in submission to the Bible. He should be caring and zealous to do God's will, turning from sin, regular in prayer, and displaying fruits of the Spirit. In short, if a Christian woman does not respect a man and if she cannot detect signs of sincere spiritual growth, she is a fool to place her heart into his hand.

The Bible's plan for marriage does more than help us to make good choices about whom we should date. It also shows us what the relationship is moving toward. God does not command women to submit to their boyfriends. But the patterns of masculine leadership and feminine help should increasingly characterize their relationship. She should be learning to encourage him while trusting to follow his lead. When there are problems, they should talk about them. (Submission does not always demand silence!) A relationship that is heading toward marriage should be one in which the woman feels an increasing trust in the man and the man feels an increasing respect for her.

This is the making of a strong partnership and a satisfying love.

In particular, when a single woman thinks of a wife's submission to her husband, she should prepare for this by practicing respect for the man she is dating. Ephesians 5:33 says, "Let the wife see that she respects her husband." This is not something magically concocted in the wedding ceremony, but something cultivated during the time of dating. To respect a man is to honor him and show appreciation. The opposite occurs when a woman is critical or complaining, and in dating this often happens when she races ahead of the man in her emotions or her demands. According to Proverbs 14:1, "The wisest of women builds her house, but folly with her own hands tears it down." So it is for a nagging, complaining woman in her relationship with a man. Just as respect and admiration is the mortar that builds up the love in his heart, disrespect is an acid that embitters a man's relationship with a woman.

> Submission in marriage implies the need for respect while dating. She learns to encourage him while trusting to following his lead.

What, then, does submission and respect look like for a woman in a dating relationship? Here are some guidelines:

1. A woman should allow the man to initiate the relationship. This does not mean that she does nothing. She helps! If she thinks there is a good possibility for a relationship, she makes herself accessible to him and helps him to make conversation, putting

him at ease and encouraging him as opportunities arise (she does the opposite when she does not have interest in a relationship with a man). A godly woman will not try to manipulate the start of a relationship, but will respond to the interest and approaches of a man in a godly, encouraging way.

2. A godly woman should speak positively and respectfully about her boyfriend, both when with him and when apart.

3. She should give honest attention to his interests and respond to his attention and care by opening up her heart.

4. She should recognize the sexual temptations with which a single man will normally struggle. Knowing this, she will dress attractively but modestly, and will avoid potentially compromising situations. She must resist the temptation to encourage sexual liberties as a way to win his heart.

5. The Christian woman should build up the man with God's Word and give encouragement to godly leadership. She should allow and seek biblical encouragement from the man she is dating.

6. She should make "helping" and "respecting" the watchwords of her behavior toward a man. She should ask herself, "How can I encourage him, especially in his walk with God?" "How can I provide practical helps that are appropriate to the current place in our relationship?" She should share with him in a way that will enable him to care for her heart, asking, "What can I do or say that will help him to understand who I really am, and how can I participate in the things he cares about?"

7. She must remember that this is a brother in the Lord. She should not be afraid to end an unhealthy

relationship, but should seek to do so with charity and grace. Should the relationship not continue forward, the godly woman will ensure that her time with a man will have left him spiritually blessed.

Conclusion

The redeemed dating relationship is one that is patterned on God's commands for a blessed marriage and that increasingly moves in that direction. Women, aware of the sinful tendency to want to usurp the man's role, should commit themselves to a renewed obedience to God's Word in submission to the Lord. Men, knowing their own tendency to treat women as objects of pleasure and aware of their responsibility before the Lord, must embrace the obligations that come with their role. They therefore nurture and protect women instead of using them to serve their own desires.

> The redeemed dating relationship is patterned on God's commands for marriage, increasingly moving in that direction. Both man and woman should commit themselves to obedience to God's Word.

Above all, we hope to have shown that sincere Christians ought to approach a dating relationship with confidence and a real hope that flows from God's Word. These two passages, Ephesians 5:22–33 and 1 Peter 3:1–7, provide a blueprint for how Christian couples can appropriate God's blessing in their marriage, as well as a pattern for how a man and a woman can grow their love in a dating relationship. God has designed the relationship between a man and a woman to work in a certain way. While each couple is different from every other in many ways—this is part of the excitement of discovery in romance—the individuals' approach to each other should always be patterned on God's design for men and women in love.

Learning to love in this way is the journey of a lifetime. Through a mutual commitment to God and his Word, couples learn how to redeem what sin destroys, enjoying blessings almost forgotten in our world with its secular, manipulative view of dating and marriage.

If marriage is a garden in which love can safely and strongly grow, the seeds of this relationship are planted and begin their growth long before the wedding ceremony. As the Christian couple seeks after marriage in a dating relationship, they should therefore aim for those dynamics that will build a strong and godly marriage. Just as a building requires a solid foundation, the patterns and attitudes developed while dating will most certainly carry over into the marriage relationship. This should give Christian men and women a sober attitude toward dating, but also a joyful desire to appropriate God's blessing from the beginning of their time together. A man and a woman in love are each given by God for the blessing of the other. Each is given by God the means to build strength and grace in the life of the other, and together in Christ they reveal the Lord's own love before the eyes of a watching world.

Learning to love is a lifetime journey.
Through God and his Word, couples learn to redeem what sin destroys, enjoying blessings that are forgotten by our secular world.

PART TWO

Biblical Wisdom for Dating and Relationships

5

Words to the Wise

A Proverbial Take on Attraction

IT IS TIME FOR US TO do a practical exercise. As you are reading this book, we want you to take out a piece of paper (or you can just write in the margins; we do that all the time). At the top of the page, write "Attraction." If you are a man, list those things that attract you to a woman. Just go ahead and put looks right at the top of the list! If you are a woman, list those things that attract you to a man. There is no point in not being honest. Think about people you have been attracted to and ask yourself what it was that caught your attention. Think about people you have found unattractive and ask yourself why.

What we're going to do in this chapter is to compare what attracts you to a person of the opposite sex with what the Bible says should attract you. We are dealing here with a much-neglected part of the Christian life, namely, wisdom. Christians are often focused on being obedient to

God, and rightly so. But few of us realize that God calls us to cultivate more than just obedience. We are to cultivate wisdom. Wisdom is good judgment about what is right and good in actual situations. The best place in the Bible to go for wisdom is, of course, the book of Proverbs. So in this chapter we will discuss what Proverbs says is wise when it comes to the matter of attraction.

The Beauty He Beholds

Our experience with Christian singles has produced a list of things men are attracted to that goes something like this, in order: looks, personality, shared interests/goals, and godly character. If you divide these four items in half, giving one woman the top two—looks and personality—and another woman the bottom two—shared interests/goals and godly character—then experience shows that lady #1 is going out to dinner and lady #2 is staying home to iron. Before we criticize this, men protest, "You don't expect me to date a woman to whom I'm not attracted, do you?" The point, however, is that what really attracts most men are those things on the surface, while those things underneath exert precious little influence.

For very many (foolish) men, the first quality—sensual appeal—overrides everything else. Sexual attraction is indeed important; the Bible's teaching on sexuality in marriage argues against a man's dating or marrying a woman he finds unappealing. But most men find more than a few women sexually appealing to at least a suitable degree. So a little consultation with the book of Proverbs might help the man to make a wise selection when finding a woman to date with an eye to marriage.

It turns out that the first thing we find in the book of Proverbs is a warning that is extremely relevant to our discussion. Proverbs 6:23–26 warns young men not to become entangled with evil women. The warning involves the very trap into which so many men are led by their eyes: "Do not desire her beauty in your heart, and do not let her capture you with her eyelashes" (Prov. 6:25). The first principle that Proverbs gives men, therefore, is to be on their guard when confronted with physical beauty in a woman. Can it be coincidental that the book of Proverbs, written especially with the training of young men in mind, concludes with this warning: "Charm is deceitful, and beauty is vain, but a woman who fears the LORD is to be praised" (Prov. 31:30)?

> For many men, sensual appeal overrides all
> other attractions. But Proverbs 6:25 warns,
> "Do not desire her beauty in your heart."

Men, let's go back to the list we asked you to make. If beauty is at the top and godliness is tagged on at the bottom, then the Bible advises you to turn your piece of paper upside down—that is, if you want to be wise, and if you want your decisions to be shaped not by the world and its desires but by God and his wisdom. What Proverbs tells us is that a man should not allow his flesh alone to do the choosing. Instead of considering those women who are most physically attractive, and then trying to restrain your flesh so as to give at least some thought to Christian character, you ought first to focus on those women who give evidence of fearing the Lord. Feminine wiles are deceiving, says God's Word, and men easily fall prey to this very thing. Therefore, a wise Christian man will protect himself from the entrapment of beauty and will desire above all else a godly, growing Christian woman.

As an aside, men need to know what Christian women are going through today. The Bible tells women to cultivate inner beauty rather than outward. Peter tells them, "Do not let your adorning be external . . . but let your adorning be the hidden person of the heart with the imperishable beauty of a gentle and quiet spirit, which in God's sight is very precious" (1 Peter 3:3–4). What a comfort those last words are to women, because such virtues are not very precious in the sight of Christian men! Too many godly women who give themselves to spiritual depth and beauty are worn down by watching the affections of Christian men go only to the pretty face and the shapely body. What a shame it is—and what an indictment on Christian masculinity—that women who trust and obey God's Word are neglected by the very men who most ought to treasure what they have inside. What a contribution it would make to the kingdom of God if Christian men were attracted to biblical virtues in women!

What a shame that women who cultivate inner beauty through God's Word are neglected by Christian men—the very men who most ought to treasure what they have.

Speaking of inner beauty, it is this that the book of Proverbs next emphasizes about a biblically attractive woman. Proverbs tells men to rule out all women who do not display godly character, preserving themselves from the folly of seduction. But specific virtues are recommended to those who wish to be happy in love with a woman. The first is *noble character.* Proverbs 12:4 (NIV) says, "A wife of noble character is her husband's crown, but a disgraceful wife is like decay in his bones." The point has to do with the way in which the woman conducts herself in her dealings with people. Does she win admiration, thus reflecting positively on her man? This reflects the way she dresses, the way she talks, the way she treats people and responds to situations, and the kinds of friends and associations she has. A woman who in these things brings shame to herself and thus contempt to her man "is like decay in his bones." Her good looks might seem worth it at first, but as the decay eats away over time, the man is embittered by the disgrace of his woman. In the classic language common to this book of wisdom, Proverbs 11:22 issues a warning heard too late by many foolish men: "Like a gold ring in a pig's snout is a beautiful woman without discretion." For such a woman, even her beauty is a disgrace, and its luster is soon tarnished by her lack of character.

Rule out all women
who do not display godly character.

A biblical example is Samson's one-time gal, Delilah, recounted in Judges 16. She was obviously beautiful (or Samson would have taken no interest), and she could probably be a lot of fun. But her associations were disgraceful. Her motives in their relationship were poisonous. Her conduct was filled with shame. Because of her, Samson lost his strength and was disgraced; so it is for any man who foolishly woos a disgraceful woman.

Delilah is an extreme example; we all should be able to avoid a woman like that. But in less extreme cases, sexual attraction can keep a man from noticing what is obvious to everyone else. Therefore, it is a good idea for a man to arrange for a prospective date to meet his friends and then take seriously what they have to say. Particularly if a dating relationship is on the brink of becoming serious, a man should observe the woman around his boss, in the company of his parents, in a conversation with his pastor. If the woman is possessed with less than a noble character, it is likely to come out in such encounters. But a woman who consistently handles such situations with grace and composure is biblically recommended to the wise Christian man.

Another virtue that Proverbs commends is *kindheartedness*. The English Standard Version of Proverbs 11:16 says, "A gracious woman gets honor." The context makes it clear that this wording is in line with the rendering of the New International Version: "A kindhearted woman gains respect." A kindly woman is one who ministers selflessly to others. She does not complain about sacrifices or make constant demands for herself. Her heart is opened outward toward the hurts and needs of others.

Nowhere is this characteristic exemplified more beautifully than in Rebekah, whom God provided to be the wife of the patriarch Isaac. Isaac's father, Abraham, sent his servant to his homeland to find a wife for his son and heir. The servant was faithful and wise, for he asked God to identify the bride-to-be by her servant heart. His plan was to go to a watering hole in the desert and ask a young woman to share with him a drink. The chosen one would be the one who replied, "Drink, and I will water your camels" (Gen. 24:12–14). God answered the servant's request to bless this plan, and he came upon Rebekah, a distant relative of Abraham's. Yes, she "was very attractive in appearance" (v. 16). But that was not the determining issue. She was at a spring, filling her jar, when the servant came to her and asked,

"Please give me a little water to drink from your jar" (v. 17). Rebekah replied out of the kindness of her heart, "Drink, my lord" (v. 18). And when he had drunk from her jar she went even further, saying, "I will draw water for your camels also, until they have finished drinking" (v. 19). She proceeded to water all his camels until they were full—and camels drink a very great deal of water. Stunned and gazing in silence, Abraham's servant realized that he had found just the wife for his master's son.

> A kindhearted woman ministers selflessly to others, without complaining about the sacrifices.

It is obvious that Rebekah was also noted for the third virtue highlighted in Proverbs, namely, *industry*. She was not afraid to work hard and was a woman who could make contributions. Proverbs 14:1 teaches, "The wisest of women builds her house, but folly with her own hands tears it down." What a godly man looks for, then, is a woman who is building, who is making, and who is contributing in positive ways. There he will find wisdom both in the woman and for himself. The contrast is clear: the opposite of an industrious woman is one who tears things down.

A woman's industry shines through chiefly in her positive attitude. Conversely, a woman who tears down typically does so with her tongue. For an argumentative or bitter woman Proverbs reserves its choicest scorn. Proverbs 19:13–14 warns—and let the wise man take heed—"A wife's quarreling is a continual dripping of rain." Is anything more destructive to a house than a leak that constantly drips? "But a prudent wife is from the LORD." Most classic of all is the exclamation of Proverbs 21:9: "It is better to live in a corner of the housetop than in a house shared with a quarrelsome wife."

Industry occupies an important place in that chapter most noted for its picture of an excellent woman, Proverbs 31. But the chief virtue celebrated here is *faithfulness*. An excellent woman is trustworthy. "The heart of her husband trusts in her, and he will have no lack of gain" (Prov. 31:11). In perusing this great chapter, a man will find all the virtues spoken of already; Proverbs 31 provides the paradigm for godly femininity. This woman's nobility shines through in fear of the Lord: "Strength and dignity are her clothing, and she laughs at the time to come. She opens her mouth with wisdom, and the teaching of kindness is on her tongue" (vv. 25–26). Her kindheartedness is praised for the blessing it brings: "She does him good, and not harm, all the days of her life" (v. 12). "Give her the fruit of her hands," it says in praise of her industry, "and let her works praise her in the gates" (v. 31).

These are the feminine virtues that the Bible commends to a wise and godly man. First, the virtuous woman fears the Lord, not relying on the deceitfulness of charm or the vanity of beauty. Then, by observing her, the wise onlooker finds nobility, kindheartedness, industry, and faithfulness. And then, what about her looks? Yes, the Bible values good looks. But the man who has gazed into a Christian woman's heart and found there things of beauty and worth will be sure to look upon her face and find loveliness there as well.

A man is not missing out by being wise! Physical beauty may entice, but it lacks power to build up and to bless. The man who truly misses out in life is the one who passes over a woman of inner, spiritual beauty. The fruit she bears nurtures a man's spirit and draws him nearer to

God. The wise man looks for such a woman to whom to give his heart (and his future children, and his bank account), and to her he can wisely make the commitments demanded by real love.

> Men miss out when they pass over women of inner, spiritual beauty. "Charm is deceitful, and beauty is vain, but a woman who fears the Lord is to be praised" (Prov. 31:30).

Beauty That Really Matters

Since we live in a sensually obsessed culture, men and women today are consumers of beauty. In one recent year, twenty billion dollars were spent on cosmetics and another thirty billion on diet products. In order to win the respect and love for which they yearn, women seek power through beauty. The rules of beauty are that a woman must never age and must maintain a perpetually thin, shapely body. The problem with beauty—outward beauty, at least—is that it is not permanent and that it has great power to seduce a person into morally harmful behavior. Physical beauty is only skin deep and is no guarantee of the greater beauty of a godly character.

Beauty is, of course, a gift from God. Indeed, beauty is one of the most precious gifts that a woman brings into a man's otherwise drab and utilitarian existence. The Song of Solomon shows a husband and wife delighting in each other, the man especially exulting in the sensual beauty of his wife. But what God intends as a gift can just as well be made a weapon of manipulation. When that happens, beauty ceases to be a blessing for either man or woman. Indeed, one of the tragedies of sin is that beauty ceases to be a good but instead becomes a god—a false god that fails to satisfy and only destroys.

Since beauty is so dangerous, should women strive to be plain and homely? Is this their mark of spirituality? Hardly! Women were made for beauty. But a wise woman bestows her beauty as a gift instead of using it as a weapon. Her beauty is from God, and she exercises it in stewardship to him.

A wise woman bestows her beauty as a gift.
Her beauty is from God, and she exercises
it in stewardship to him.

A steward is a caretaker. Women should thus care for their beauty—inwardly and outwardly. A steward also guards and protects. Therefore, a woman should be modest with her beauty. We have often heard Christian women complain that men seem interested only in their bodies. But we have wanted to ask them, "What are you using to attract these men? Is it not just that—your bodies?" A woman who dresses sensually should not be surprised to learn that the men she attracts are driven mainly by the eyes and the flesh.

A steward is also careful in the use of her resources. In respect to physical beauty, women need to realize that a great many single men—yes, Christians, too—struggle with lust. The Bible says, "Love your neighbor as yourself" (Rom. 13:9), and a Christian woman loves her single brothers by dressing and acting modestly. Frankly, styles of clothing popular today are designed to outline and highlight those parts of a woman's body that are especially attractive to men. But a modest woman considers how her clothing presents her body and what her motive is for wearing any particular style. This does not call for a sanctified frumpiness—a woman may dress modestly and attractively. The Bible says, "Women should adorn themselves in respectable apparel, with modesty and self-control, . . . with what is proper for women who profess godliness—with good works" (1 Tim. 2:9–10).

The good news for women is that God offers a beauty that is so much greater and more satisfying than mere sensual beauty. God offers a beauty that won't fade when you grow old or even when you die, a beauty that you can take with you all the way to heaven. This beauty is best explained by the apostle Peter in one of the Bible's great passages on marriage:

> Wives, be subject to your own husbands, so that even if some do not obey the word, they may be won without a word by the conduct of their wives—when they see your respectful and pure conduct. Do not let your adorning be external—the braiding of hair, the wearing of gold, or the putting on of clothing—but let your adorning be the hidden person of the heart with the imperishable beauty of a gentle and quiet spirit, which in God's sight is very precious. For this is how the holy women who hoped in God used to adorn themselves. . . . (1 Peter 3:1–5)

Here is a beauty that never comes in a jar! Instead, it comes in a heart that is turned toward God and in which his light is shining. It is a beauty that has the power to draw men not merely to itself but also to God. Peter is writing to women whose husbands are not believers; his counsel is for women to exhibit the glory of God through the purity of their inner selves. His concern is not to forbid outward beauty itself—for all true beauty is of God—but rather its abuse. The godly woman cultivates "the imperishable beauty of a gentle and quiet spirit, which in God's sight is very precious." These are not personality traits, but fruits of the Holy Spirit of God as he grows in a believing woman's heart.

God offers a beauty that won't fade when you grow old and that you can take with you all the way to heaven.

So here is the question: Will you lose out if you pursue this kind of beauty? Will all the guys pass you by for women whose beauty is all on the surface? Will it pay to cultivate the beauty commanded by God instead of that commanded by the billboards and television ads? Is God able and willing to provide what you need? If not, then we really shouldn't believe or trust in him. But if he is, then what freedom we have! Men and women alike have freedom to do what is right, to pursue what is best, and to cultivate that which is most beautiful: the imperishable beauty of the heart.

Specifically, God's Word says a woman is beautiful when she is *gentle* or *meek*. This is not the same as weakness, even though many people think so today. A woman becomes gentle when she learns to act not in self-assertion or self-interest, but in reliance on God to provide all that she needs. She is less self-reliant and more God-reliant. She does not hide her abilities, but offers them up to God's sovereign control. Feminine beauty is furthermore *quiet*. This refers to a peace or tranquility arising from within. It is a peace that comes from trusting God's promises and knowing God's character. This kind of inner beauty finds its resources and hope in God alone.

Peter makes a telling comment at the end of this great passage on feminine beauty. Having compared such women to Abraham's wife, Sarah, he adds, "You are her daughters, if you do good and do not fear . . ." (1 Peter 3:6). Now, when it comes to beauty, what does a woman have to fear? So much! She fears time. She fears competition. She fears the fickle hearts of shallow men. She fears the wear and tear of life. Ah, but the woman whose beauty is within, who relies on the Lord alone for her portion and her cup—what does she have to fear? Nothing. She believes Psalm 34:10: "Those who seek the LORD lack no good thing." Here is a women's liberation of which the world knows nothing! The woman who does not give in to fear, who is not intimidated by the ads, and who is not discouraged by the baser motives of men has the privilege of possessing a beauty that is higher than any other, that is precious to the Lord, and that will never fade away.

One particularly obnoxious television ad promoted beauty with close-up shots of a woman's luscious lips, reddened to perfection by the expensive lipstick being promoted. Its line read, "What do your lips say?" That is, indeed, a valuable gauge of true beauty. In great measure, the lips declare a woman's beauty, not in their allure to a foolish man but in how they reveal the character of her heart. Jesus taught, "Out of the overflow of the heart the mouth speaks" (Matt. 12:34, NIV). That means that a Christian woman who wants to display true beauty will cultivate her heart and express it through her speech. Remember what the proverb said about a quarrelsome woman—that a man would be better off living on a corner of a roof than under it with her. A woman's gentleness and quietness of spirit will be revealed through gracious, godly speech that builds up and does not tear down.

> A woman's beauty—her gentleness
> and quietness of spirit—is revealed through
> her gracious, godly speech.

Earlier in this chapter, we considered what a wise and biblically informed man should seek in a wife. Isn't that the kind of man you want to be attracted to you? Take a look, then, at what you are presenting to men and ask what kind of man you will attract. If you are relying on charm and outward beauty, setting them forth in your dress and flirtatious conduct, then realize that it is only the foolish man who will fall into your trap. Especially if you are loud or contentious, realize that the Bible specifically warns men against falling for you. The godly man, the man who will make a loving and faithful husband, sees you and turns away. How much better for you to trust the Lord and cultivate those spiritual beauties that are calculated to draw a man of godly character and real wisdom and, better still, that are certain to make you precious in the sight of our loving Lord and God.

Blessed Is the Man

A woman is terribly mistaken if she trusts in outward beauty alone. But she is also mistaken if she believes that just any man will do. So what does the Bible have to say about the kind of man a godly woman should want? First, let's go back to the list that you gals were supposed to make at the beginning of this chapter. What did you put at the top of that list?

It is a commonplace fact that women are not motivated by looks as much as men are. This is to their blessing because a pretty face can be just as dangerous to a woman as it is to a man! According to one secular survey, what women most desire in a man is, first, financial security and then intelligence, followed by personality and physical appearance.[1] If one word sums up what women look for, that word is *confidence*. When a man carries himself like someone important, is assertive and decisive, and is looked up to by others, women are likely to find him attractive. The problem is that a man may exude confidence without possessing a godly character. Just as the foolish man falls for a pretty face without thinking about what lies beneath, so also does the foolish woman swoon over a charming man without considering whether she is safe in his hands.

> A man may exude confidence without a godly character. A foolish woman swoons over a charming man without considering whether she is safe in his hands.

What does Proverbs tell a woman who wishes to be wise in her choice of a man? The place to begin is in his relationship to the Lord. Proverbs 8:34 says, "Blessed is the one who listens to me, watching daily at my gates, waiting beside my doors." The first thing this tells a Christian woman is to seek a man who is regular at church. There are few more important indicators of a man's spiritual maturity than his frequency in worship with God's people. Of course, a Christian is forbidden by God to marry a non-Christian; this effectively rules out dating with unbelievers as well (see again 1 Cor. 7:39; 2 Cor. 6:14). But a believing man who often cannot make time to faithfully attend and to be a contributing member of a church is not a likely candidate for the obligations and challenges of marriage. In our years of ministering to single Christians, we often heard laments from women who dated marginally committed Christian men who were otherwise quite attractive. These are the men who want to snuggle close on Saturday night but are nowhere in sight on Sunday morning. We remember one woman in particular who finally told her beau, "I would rather we be together on Sunday than on Saturday." Thankfully, the woman was mature enough to anticipate the problems with such a relationship, and it soon came to an end.

The kind of man that a Christian woman wants is a man of the Word of God, a man of prayer, and a man who delights in worship. Proverbs 14:26 (NIV) sums it up: "He who fears the LORD has a secure fortress, and for his children it will be a refuge." Far more important in a man than money, than charisma, and than all the other things the world values is a heart that is turned toward the Lord.

A Christian woman should want a man
of the Word, a man of prayer, and
a man who delights in worship.

The classic biblical bad example is King Saul, Israel's first king. The people foolishly demanded that God give them a king who would be impressive in the eyes of men

(1 Sam. 8:5). God relented, acting in judgment by giving them just what they wanted: "Saul, a handsome young man. . . . From his shoulders upward he was taller than any of the people" (1 Sam. 9:2). Saul had looks and strength; Saul had drive and ability. The only thing Saul lacked was a heart that feared the Lord, and as a result he led the people astray. When God finally replaced him, he was gracious enough to give "a man after his own heart" (1 Sam. 13:14). When David was selected as the new and true king, despite his youth and humility, the Lord spoke words that should be remembered by us all: "Man looks on the outward appearance, but the LORD looks on the heart" (1 Sam. 16:7). Instead of wanting a man who has it all, a Christian woman should seek and pray for one who, for all his weaknesses and failings, is a man after God's own heart.

Just as Proverbs commends specific character traits in women, God's book of wisdom has much to say about the characteristics found in a genuinely desirable man. First among these is *industry*, one of the very qualities so prized in women. This is especially important in a man, who will normally be called to provide for his family. Proverbs 10:4 says, "A slack hand causes poverty, but the hand of the diligent makes rich." This is why it is important for a woman to know about a man's work—and, most importantly, his attitude toward his work. From the beginning, God intended for men to be hard workers who build and protect (see again Gen. 2:15). Many men falsely pursue success and glory through their work, and this is idolatry. But there is such a thing as godly ambition, and a man ought to desire to improve his family's circumstances and to accomplish things in his work. Likewise, a woman ought to observe how a man handles his money to see whether he is thinking about the future or only the moment's pleasure. As Proverbs 12:27 says, "Whoever is slothful will not roast his game, but the diligent man will get precious wealth."

Furthermore, a woman should seek a man of *integrity*. According to Proverbs 10:9, "Whoever walks in integrity walks securely, but he who makes his ways crooked will be found out." This was King Saul's chief problem; he was willing to do what was expedient rather than what was right. A man who is dishonest at work, who is not careful to keep his word, or who lacks the courtesy to show up on time does not commend himself as one likely to be faithful and reliable in marriage.

A man who is dishonest at work, is not careful to keep his word, or lacks the courtesy to show up on time does not commend himself as one likely to be faithful and reliable in marriage.

Numerous proverbs speak in one way or another of *self-control*. For example, hear this advice from Proverbs 11:12: "Whoever belittles his neighbor lacks sense, but a man of understanding remains silent." The way a man speaks to and about others says much about his character. Proverbs 16:32 tells us, "Whoever is slow to anger is better than the mighty, and he who rules his spirit than he who takes a city." Indeed, any man who is quick to anger and often critical, especially if he speaks more harshly and is more demanding as the relationship goes along, is to be shunned by a woman every bit as much as a disagreeable woman is to be shunned by a man.

Not surprisingly, Proverbs has fine things to say about a man who shows *kindness*. Proverbs 11:17 teaches, "A man who is kind benefits himself, but a cruel man hurts himself." Moreover, "Whoever brings blessing will be enriched, and one who waters will himself be watered" (Prov. 11:25). We have already seen that a loving marriage requires a husband to minister with care and attentiveness to his wife; a woman ought to look for kindness and a heart that freely ministers with a thoughtful word and an attentive ear.

A man who is often angry and critical is to be shunned by women. Look for kindness and a heart that freely ministers with a thoughtful word and an attentive ear.

Two men from the Bible whom we might profitably compare are Samson and Boaz, who probably lived around the same time. What can we say about Samson? He epitomizes fleshly attraction. He was practically the strongest man ever, and success followed where he went. And confidence—if all you want is a strapping, confident, impressive man, then Samson is the one for you! One thing we know for sure about Samson: he didn't have trouble winning the hearts of women! But Samson was also something like a walking billboard of flashing red lights from the book of Proverbs. He bounced from job to job and spent all his money as soon as he got it. His word was good for nothing, and he made up the rules as he went along. As for self-control, who needs it when nobody is able to stand up to you? Samson may have had some kindness, but as he runs through women and runs over men, it doesn't show up much in the Bible. Samson was the kind of man who could turn out right only by destroying himself—which is exactly what happened. It makes for quite the biblical hero, but not for the type of man that a woman should want to attract.

Compared to Samson, Boaz is a little-known figure in the Bible. He was, however, a man of some local stature in Bethlehem. We learn about him through the eyes of Ruth, a foreign-born woman without money or status. She was completely vulnerable in the man's world that was the ancient Near East. But Ruth's nobility shone through in her willingness to glean the leftovers from the fields in order to provide food for her beloved mother-in-law. She happened upon the field of Boaz, who inquired about her. There is little doubt that Boaz could have secured rights to Ruth had he wanted to, but instead he kindly gave her permission and gave her provision of water as well. When asked why he showed this foreign woman such favor, Boaz revealed that he had noticed her character: "All that you have done for your mother-in-law since the death of your husband has been fully told to me," he explained (Ruth 2:11). As the story goes on, Ruth decided to make herself available to Boaz's attentions. It turns out, as well, that Boaz was a distant relative of Ruth's deceased husband. When called upon to pay the money required to make good on Ruth's obligations, Boaz faithfully accepted his responsibility. He feared the Lord, was a man who worked hard for attainments in life, and was honest, faithful, and kind. It is no surprise that this was a match made in heaven, and many of Ruth's and Boaz's finer qualities resurfaced in their more celebrated descendant, King David.

And You're Not Such a Peach Yourself!

We want to conclude this chapter with a word of balance: as you consider the godly virtues of prospective husbands and wives, remember that no one is perfect. God has no woman, or no man, for you who is anything but a redeemed sinner being transformed by the Holy Spirit. The whole point of Christian marriage is for two vastly flawed people to grow in the Lord together while they are taught how to love by a gracious God.

> Remember, no one is perfect. Christian marriage is for two vastly flawed people to grow in the Lord together.

One of our frustrations in ministering to singles is the tendency for a Christian man or woman to produce a checklist of likes and dislikes, as advised in a multitude of books on dating. But there is a world of difference between the approach we have advocated—that you seek godly character traits as commended in the Bible—and the selfish pursuit of someone to satisfy all your wants and match all your preferences. The problem with the latter approach, in our view, is twofold. On the one hand, marriage is not based on compatibility. Sure, it is great to be with someone who is basically just like you. But apparent compatibility in dating often evaporates under the more revealing light of marriage. It is good to be wise in the matter of attraction. But as we have tried to show in this book, what matters more is your willingness to love. In the end, the only compatibility that really matters is a shared faith in

Christ and a mutual commitment to his Word as it teaches you to love.

Marriage is based not on compatibility,
but on your willingness to love.

The second problem is one we have had to point out to many a smug, checklist-wielding single—dismayed at the absence of the perfect man or woman. To them we have had to reply, "You're not such a peach yourself!" So if you are a person who needs grace and patience and charity—and you are!—then wisdom suggests that you offer this same kind of love to a man or woman who is just as flawed as you. So by all means be wise when it comes to love! But model your love on the example of God, who "shows his love for us in that while we were still sinners, Christ died for us" (Rom. 5:8).

6

Table for Two

The First Date

WE BEGAN THIS BOOK with the question, "What does the Bible say about dating?" We are now halfway through, and we have not even talked about going on a date! The reason is that we first needed to understand God's design for male–female relationships, along with how sin affects—and then how God's grace in Christ redeems—our relationships. We also needed to dig for some biblical wisdom on the matter of attraction. So we are finally ready to start talking about actual dates!

What does the Bible say about dates themselves? For starters, it gives us lots of examples, such as those found in the book of Judges. Samson knew a lot about dating, but his example is not one that most of us want to follow. In Judges chapter 21, the elders of the tribe of Benjamin gave this counsel to their single men: "Go and lie in ambush in the vineyards and watch. If the daughters of

Shiloh come out to dance in the dances, then come out of the vineyards and snatch each man his wife from the daughters of Shiloh, and go to the land of Benjamin" (vv. 20–21). This plan actually worked, but it is not one that Christian men should expect God to bless (nor did it please God at the time). Moving to a more uplifting portion of Scripture, the book of Ruth provides one of the Bible's great love stories. But the model of dating presented there is probably not helpful for singles today. Boaz dated Ruth by allowing her to glean leftovers from his fields, and she made her interest in him known by lying at his feet as he slept on the threshing floor. There is much to be learned about redeeming love from the book of Ruth, but its dating practices are not much help for the Christian single today.

The point is that we do not live in the social world that provided us the Bible.

So what can Scripture tell us about dating in the social reality of our time? Here, as before, we can apply biblical principles that will help us to honor God and develop healthy relationships. In this chapter we will take that approach in offering practical advice for dating. How does a Christian ask someone out? What advice do we have for first dates? How should you act and what should you do afterwards?

Hold That Phone!

Few aspects of dating involve more stress and confusion than the first date. How many promising relationships have never even begun or have gotten off on the wrong foot because of the anguish surrounding this tortured exercise. Furthermore, here is an element of male–female relationships that has changed perhaps more than any other in recent decades. It wasn't too long ago that what amounted to a first date took place in the young lady's parlor, under the close supervision of her mother. Back then, it was the woman who initiated the relationship; a young man could dare come calling only if first invited to receive her attention—and there might be many young men so encouraged! The whole point of that more genteel system was the protection of the woman—the protection of her virtue, of her reputation, and of her heart. But how things have changed! And how often our current practices expose women, who find themselves in intimate settings with men whom neither they nor their families or friends really know and may not approve of if they did.

Nostalgia will do us little good. We may pine for more ordered days, when social life had real conventions, and we may even succeed in renewing some worthy practices. Thus, the recent emphasis on courtship has entered the picture. Many would advocate that a Christian man seeking a relationship with a Christian woman ought first to approach her father for consent, advice, and oversight. There is little to say against this idea, given the Bible's teaching on a father's headship over his family. When possible, we strongly encourage men to follow this model. The problem for many today, however, is that their families are broken or distant or do not have strong biblical views regarding relationships.

However we do it, here is a matter in which Christians ought truly to be countercultural. We are living in a time when the boundaries and fences guarding social life have been removed, with the so-called liberation of so many facets of life. The cost has been high, as our society has bought into sinful patterns that hurt everyone and that especially expose women to exploitation. Women today are encouraged to wander alone into the arms of romance;

for many, the result is the loss of their purity and the ravaging of their emotions. Also involved is the radical individualism of contemporary life. Whereas the Bible considers us in terms of the bonds of family and covenant relationships, it seldom crosses the minds of people today that their affairs are more than private matters. Under this way of thinking, a young man and woman meet: he wants to have a good time, and she wants to feel loved. They resent the idea that they are accountable to a broader community. This is the way life works in steamy novels and television shows, in which people have their ups and downs but everyone ends up happy. But in reality, this approach encourages social behaviors that stand in the way of healthy dating relationships.

Based on the Bible's teaching, we suggest some principles and practices that may vastly improve the experience of dating. First, the Bible tells us to show "honor to the woman as the weaker vessel" (1 Peter 3:7). While both men and women should take steps to be prudent and wise, women are especially vulnerable in romantic relationships. For this reason, a woman ought not to be exposed to a date—that is, a romantic, one-on-one social outing—with a man whose character is unknown. (Remember the previous chapter, when we emphasized the importance of godly character!) If a largely unknown man approaches a woman to go on a date, and if she thinks she might be interested, she ought to suggest some mixed setting in which she can get to know him, perhaps attending a social function as part of a larger group. In the meantime, the woman would be wise to make discreet inquiries with people whose counsel she trusts. Ideally, this would be her father, given the Bible's teaching that an unmarried woman is under her father's care (see 1 Cor. 11:3[1]); or in the absence of her father it could be her pastor, or at the very least trustworthy friends.

First and foremost, the man must be a committed believer; a Christian woman has no business dating a non-Christian man (and vice versa—see 1 Cor. 7:39; 2 Cor. 6:14). Even if he is a professing believer, how often we have seen a woman go out with a man who was widely known as an absolute cad. She might have easily discovered this by asking any number of people. The point is that a woman needs to know about a man's background and character before he has worked his way into her heart. This simple practice goes a long way toward protecting Christian women from predatory men, and it also helps in starting a relationship well.

> First and foremost, the man must be
> a committed believer (1 Cor. 7:39; 2 Cor. 6:14).

Related to this is the principle that a first date between Christians should not take place incognito. Godly friends on both sides should be aware of the relationship to give counsel, to pray for blessing, and to provide accountability. If the woman is living near her parents, it would be even better for a man to approach her father first, or if that is not possible, to approach his or her pastor for godly counsel and support. The point is that when a man is out with a Christian woman, he must remember that she is someone who belongs in a community, a family, and a church. She is precious in God's sight (as is he), and because she is a sheep in Christ's flock, her well-being is of great concern to those called to shepherd. This need not make dating a heavy or onerous experience; rather, it simply puts it in a safe and godly perspective. Given a biblical knowledge of human sinfulness and the obligation of parents and the church to protect those who are vulnerable—and while single women are not helpless children, they certainly are vulnerable when it comes to dating—it is mind-boggling that Christians should permit anything less.

If this advice seems excessive, let us remember the Bible's teaching on the reality of sin. Christian women can and should be admirable for their strength of faith and character, but they are still in a position of social and emotional (not to mention physical) vulnerability when it comes to romantic encounters. Surely, when Malachi 2:14–16 chastises the men of Israel for dishonoring their wives, the same principle requires that we preserve the honor of Christian women before marriage and that we take reasonable steps to protect them from harm. Furthermore, to be frank, adult men and women are both sexually tempted when alone with an attractive counterpart of the opposite sex. One of the reasons why so many fall into sexual sin—bringing guilt into the relationship and short-circuiting its emotional and spiritual growth—is that they place themselves in tempting situations. This is simply foolish, and Christian men and women who are realistic about sexual temptation will not put themselves in a position to fall.

Adult men and women are both sexually tempted when alone with an attractive counterpart. You are foolish to place yourself in a tempting situation.

We want to stress three tools for godly dating: counsel, prayer, and accountability. If you want to do the right thing—right before God and right for a healthy love relationship—then you should seek biblical counsel. (We hope that is why you are reading this book.) But you should also discuss your plans for a date with someone you trust: a friend, a pastor, or a parent. Does your interest in a woman, or a man's interest in you, seem wise? (We cannot tell you how many times we could have told an amorous guy that the woman in view was very much not interested—and vice versa—or that for some other reason asking her out was a bad idea, if only we had been asked.) What about your plans for the first date? Share them with someone you trust and who cares about you. Pray about it, and talk through your intentions with God. Lastly, be accountable to someone for your conduct—not just sexually, but socially and spiritually as well—to help ensure that you handle the date rightly. Counsel, prayer, and accountability—these are three vital tools for healthy, wholesome dating.

> Counsel, prayer, and accountability—these are three vital tools for healthy, wholesome dating.

Modern and Postmodern Dating Questions

This leads to the perennial question, "Can a woman ask out a guy?" Many Christian men are put off by this kind of forwardness, and given the Bible's model of male leadership, this is not surprising. But there is nothing wrong with a woman's letting the proper channels know that she would welcome a certain man's interest. Maybe she gets a group together to go hiking or holds a dinner party in her home, where she provides herself opportunities to get to know a certain man. Remember that Eve was given to help poor Adam, and so many of our guys need a great deal of help piercing the fog of predating rituals! As we have seen throughout this discussion, it helps so much for Christian singles to be part of a godly church, with pastors and friends to help out when needed.

Some other first-date questions center on the increasingly popular idea of group dating. The intent is that Christian singles should socially interact in larger groups of men and women. As we observed above, this can be a good way for a relationship to begin if the man and woman do not know each other well. A group social event should rightly be seen as a prelude to dating, and it is often wise. But there are potential problems. We have noticed that some men never move beyond the group-dating scene; they constantly enjoy low-level affections from a wide variety of Christian sisters, never settling on any one for a more substantial relationship. And once a dating relationship has begun to move forward, how a couple acts in group social settings is very important. If the woman sees the man flirting with potential replacements, groups settings can cause a great deal of insecurity and harm the relationship. The point is that as an approach to dating, group dates are best at the very beginning of a relationship. Once a couple has developed a certain level of commitment and intimacy, those dynamics should continue when they are together with others. In short, group dates are best as a prelude to actual dating, allowing both the man and the woman to get to know each other well enough to know whether to take things further.

So should a first date be conducted alone? Well, it isn't really a date if all your friends are there. When going on a first date, a couple might wisely go out with another couple they enjoy and respect, but they might also go out alone. It is often best to avoid demanding settings, such as a company party or a college reunion. These are stressful enough for married couples! A first date should be safe, relaxing, and fun. It should minimize awkward, compromising scenes. We think it best if the first date not take place at night, both to create a more casual setting and to minimize sexual tension. The goal is to get to know each other better and to begin the process of sharing that, Lord willing, may lead to a closer relationship down the road.

> A first date should be safe, relaxing,
> and fun. Get to know each other better
> and begin the process of sharing.

Our first date was for lunch in a casual restaurant near Sharon's workplace. We talked about our families and our jobs, about our respective churches and the way the Lord was working in our lives. We parted after I walked her to work, with both of us looking forward to spending more time together and to getting to know each other better. It is one of the fondest memories we have, and it forged the first links of friendship and respect that headed us toward marriage.

Here's another question related to first dates: "Is it okay for a man and a woman to hang out together a lot when they have no romantic interest in one another?" First of all, if you are part of a nonromantic male–female couple, who enjoy each other's company and are emotionally connected, and yet neither of you has romantic aspirations for the relationship, you are the first one of these we have ever encountered

121

in years of experience with Christian singles. For this reason and others, we recommend against the practice of adult men and women "just hanging out together." For women, it involves an intimacy that is often unwise, given that the man has expressed little commitment and uncertain intentions. Meanwhile, other men who might have interest will be put off, being naturally uneasy and unsure about interfering in such a situation. Especially working women should beware of "hanging out with the boys," for the simple reason that they start acting like the boys. Our tour of Proverbs indicated clearly enough that a wise man is naturally inclined to show interest in a woman with feminine qualities, and such things are not easily cultivated in male society.

For a man, the danger is somewhat different. Many adult men pursue "friendships" with women because they feel a need for feminine companionship but aren't willing to make the commitment necessary for marriage. But marriage is what most of them really need! Hanging out with a female friend may be an effective coping strategy against loneliness, but it is often too good a coping strategy in that it interferes with God's desire for a man's maturity. Furthermore, for both the man and the woman, even a platonic relationship is likely to cause complications if a real dating relationship comes along. Jealousy, in proper proportions, is a biblically approved attitude toward one's potential spouse, and in the real world the casual guy or gal friend is no help to a healthy romance.

Many adult men pursue "friendships"
with women because they need feminine
companionship but aren't willing
to commit to marriage.

About a month after we started dating, we went on a skiing trip with a large group of Sharon's college friends. It is a miracle that our relationship survived it! Rick felt threatened by Sharon's many beloved guy friends, and she thought her nice-guy boyfriend was acting like a jerk. Whatever this says about our spiritual maturity at the time, experience with ourselves and with others has warned us about the danger to a growing romantic relationship of close "platonic" friendships.

Dressed for Success

Finally, let's give some advice to both the man and the woman about first dates. First, for the man. Be polite, well dressed, and on time. All of these things show respect and consideration. Don't be so intent on impressing her with worldly things, such as your car and the money you can spend, at least if you are hoping for the kind of woman commended in the Bible. Take her to a place that will make her feel comfortable and safe. Take an interest in her, and don't talk all the time. Ask her questions and listen to what she says in reply. You should be interested in getting to know her heart and the character of her relationship to Christ. Above all, our Lord commands you: "Love your neighbor as yourself" (Matt. 19:19). Your guiding rule should be to ensure that a woman who spends time with you is spiritually encouraged by the experience. You must take responsibility to ensure that conversation is wholesome and godly. Remember that you are out either with your future wife or with the future wife of some other Christian man. Start honoring marriage now (Heb. 13:4), and thus honor God. If this is not the woman whom God has for you to marry, then assume that her future husband may be on a first date with your future wife. Do unto him as you would have him do unto you.

> Men: Make her feel comfortable and safe. Take an interest in her, and don't talk all the time. Ensure that she is spiritually encouraged by the experience.

What is the commitment level on a first date? It is low—brother and sister in Christ. This certainly calls for care and respect. But it does not make it appropriate or wise for you to share your dirty laundry and open wide your heart. A first date is for wholesome interaction and the beginnings of a relationship, and it should not have the features of intimacy that are safe only in a more committed relationship. This, of course, means that there should be no sexual contact, and a godly man communicates respect for a woman's character by making no such advances or innuendos.

One last thing for the guys: call her the next day or evening. A woman feels tremendous anxiety about a first date, even if she isn't very much interested in the man. Express appreciation for the time you had together, and communicate to her where you think things stand. That's right—it's what you must do to protect her heart. If you are sure that you have no further interest, then graciously let her know that. How about this: "I enjoyed the time we spent together, but I don't think I'm really interested in going out again." Is that cruel? It may not be good news to her, but if it is true, then it is godly and gracious. How much better this is than giving polite but false impressions that may encourage her to cherish false hopes. (Here again is the value of having first spoken with her father, pastor, or friends. If telling her yourself will be too painful, you can let these people know and it may be easier for both of you. But if you really are not interested, you have an obligation to communicate this fact in some gracious, clear manner.) If, on the other hand, you really want to continue pursuing a relationship, you should indicate that as well. This kind of follow-up to a first date is more than a courtesy; it is the reasonable duty of any thoughtful Christian man.

Now for the woman: here is your first date advice. Remember that God wants you to help this man, and he probably needs it! Many men will be awkward and nervous on a first date, so do everything you can to be encouraging and friendly. Dress attractively, appropriately, and modestly (unless you really are hoping to attract a cad). Immodest dress or suggestive conversation is nothing less than an attempt to manipulate his interest. Women who do this incite men to lust and cause them to stumble, while starting the relationship on a very poor footing. Furthermore, do not be demanding or critical and do not complain (remember Prov. 21:9), and speak in a careful and edifying manner. Take an interest in him and get to know things about his life—his family, his work, and his interests. Speak freely about your faith and inquire about his.

> Women: God wants you to help the man,
> and he probably needs it! Be encouraging
> and friendly. Dress attractively,
> but modestly. Take an interest in him,
> and speak freely about your faith.

125

Women, too, need to remember the appropriate level of commitment and intimacy on a first date. Guard your heart and your expectations. Do not enter into a first date dreaming about marriage or trying out his last name with your first name; be emotionally prepared for it not to work out. One of the reasons the Christian man may be uneasy about dating is that the risk is too high among many other believers. If he doesn't end up marrying her, his name will be mud with all the other women at church! Such a man fears to date lest he be forced to leave a church he loves. This kind of situation is unreasonable and unfair; the woman can help by keeping expectations in check and allowing the man to interact with her without easily breaking her heart. But insist that he treat you with respect and care, and do the same to him in return. Like the man, you should resolve that time he spends in your company will have been to his spiritual blessing and will have been pleasing to the Lord. If you don't want to go out again, be honest. But don't tell your friends about the things you found unattractive; protect his reputation and cover his flaws in love.

The Time of Our Lives

We look back on our first date as one of the most special times in our lives. It is a memory we cherish together, and the fastest three-hour lunch we ever ate. So while we want you to be wise, we also want you to have fun! How enjoyable it is to spend time getting to make a more personal acquaintance with a guy or a gal you find attractive. How delightful if your first date can be something special that you can share together. So our last piece of advice is an important one: make the date something to savor and to remember. Try to relax and enjoy the person you are with. Be godly, be wise, and be thoughtful. But be yourself, too. Obviously, you want to put your best foot forward. The best way to do that is to let your date see the real you and the real Christ living in you. Psalm 37:4 says, "Delight yourself in the LORD, and he will give you the desires of your heart." So let God be sovereign, and rejoice in his goodness. Delight yourself in the privilege and the blessing of a first date, take care of your brother or sister's heart, and God will take care of yours.

> Make the date something to savor
> and remember. Relax and enjoy
> the person you are with. Let your date
> see the real you and the real Christ in you.

7

The Big C-Word

To Commit or Not to Commit?

SOMEWHERE BETWEEN FIRST spending time together and becoming engaged to be married, a man and a woman must normally have a relationship. In one way or another, the couple is *dating*. In our ministry to singles over the years, we have observed the way in which so many couples avoid this term. (We have also found that people who struggle to use this word often struggle to have successful relationships.) For a while, it was in fashion to say, "We're spending time together" instead of "We're dating." Sometimes we replied, "We're spending time together, too—we're married with five kids!" Our point is that, like it or not, our language needs a term to describe the situation of a man and a woman who are not married and are not yet betrothed, but who are involved in a romantic relationship that involves some level of exclusivity. The word for this in the English language is *dating*. This is a social phenomenon in our culture that most of us will pass through on the way to marriage, and we believe it is a relationship that can be conducted in a godly and spiritually productive manner.

First Things First

In thinking about the dating relationship, we recognize the value of our earlier study of Genesis chapter 2. We noted three key dynamics of the male–female relationship as God created it: commitment, intimacy, and interdependence. These dynamics express themselves in trust, sharing, and oneness, which are the building blocks of a love relationship that grows toward marriage. In our view, it is in these terms that the "dating game" may be played in a biblically faithful and fruitful manner, resulting either in a godly marriage or in a breakup that minimizes emotional damage. We propose that a dating relationship grows toward marriage as commitment, intimacy, and interdependence increase in godly and healthy ways. But as with everything else in life, first things come first, and that means that commitment must come before intimacy and interdependence.

A dating relationship grows toward marriage as commitment, intimacy, and interdependence increase in godly and healthy ways. Commitment comes first.

Let's go back to the first date. All the dynamics are low at this point, as we noted above. It is simply unwise to divulge all the secrets of your heart or to demand a high degree of commitment at this point. But what happens as the couple gets together a second and then a third and a fourth time?

The first thing that must happen is for the commitment issue to be addressed. A couple is dating when they have agreed to invest their time, effort, and emotions in an exclusive relationship. For us, this happened after we had spoken on the phone many times and had gone out on our third date. We went to see a movie, and afterwards Rick said something like this: "Listen, we've gone out three times now, and I think we have really started to get to know each other. I don't know exactly how far this is headed, but if you are willing I'd like for us to start a relationship and to see what the Lord will do between us." Sharon responded positively, and we became a dating couple. We were still getting to know each other, but a committed, exclusive relationship was established in which intimacy and interdependence could safely grow.

We have told that story dozens of times and have found that it really strikes a chord with most singles. Many single women who hear it begin to swoon. They say, "What I would give to have a man step forward and volunteer a level of commitment!" Many of them have never dated a Christian man who was willing to face up to the matter of commitment. In most cases, that is why they are still single! Many women feel that they must coerce even a conversation about commitment, and their experience bears this out. But for a dating relationship to move forward in a healthy, godly way, the man must be willing to take the lead in a discussion about the commitment level of the relationship.

Many women feel that they must coerce
even a conversation about commitment.
Men must take the lead in discussing
their level of commitment.

Let's make some observations at this key juncture. There is no set time frame in which commitment must be established. The point is that there is always a certain level of commitment and that this should be clearly established and understood. As the relationship changes, there is a need for a changed definition of commitment. Every relationship is different, but every relationship has a need for honest communication and the clearing of expectations about commitment. In general, we believe that sooner is better—either in committing to each other or in breaking off the relationship. The worst of all scenarios is the ill-defined commitment that drags on for months and years.

Why is this so important? Because, as we saw in our study of Genesis 2, commitment is the vessel in which a proper degree of intimacy and sharing may be safely enjoyed. As intimacy begins to grow, as it often will when a Christian man and woman who share an attraction spend time together, there will be a corresponding need for the commitment to be defined and expressed. This is the first point: if the relationship is moving forward so that intimacy is growing, the commitment issue must be defined.

To Commit or Not to Commit

Earlier we mentioned some tools that can make all the difference to a relationship: counsel, prayer, and accountability. Counsel includes wisdom from God's Word, as well as the biblical counsel we receive from a pastor, elder, parent, or friend. If you lack clarity about the wisdom of becoming more committed, then you should seek such counsel. Proverbs 12:15 says, "The way of a fool is right in his own eyes, but a wise man listens to advice." Some of the questions you might ask include: "Does this person encourage me in godliness? Am I being realistic in my expectations? (If you are waiting for the "perfect person," you are going to wait forever—and remember, you're not such a peach yourself!) What have I learned about the person's character? Is my reluctance to commit based on biblical or worldly considerations? Is there a problem with the relationship, or do I just have a problem with committing?" Talk about these things with a pastor or parent or friend—this is what they are for! If those who know and love you (and, it's to be hoped, the other person as well) express serious doubts about the relationship—or if they are excited for your prospects together—you will be wise to take their reaction seriously.

> Counsel, prayer, and accountability:
> three key tools in making decisions
> about the relationship.

One good diagnostic question to pursue has to do with your motive in either wanting commitment or fearing it: "Do I feel this way because I am trusting God or because I am not? Am I being acted upon by faith or by unbelief?" In some cases, trusting God will cause you to break up. How many bad relationships are foolishly held together because of fear—fear of loneliness, failure, or rejection. In such cases, commitment to a bad relationship is based on an unwillingness to trust the Lord. If the counsel of God's Word and of trusted advisers speaks against committing, then you should trust God enough to end the relationship. On the other hand, too many people are paralyzed by their lack of trust in God so that they never commit even to potentially wonderful partners.

This is something you ought to pray about. James 1:5 says, "If any of you lacks wisdom, let him ask God, who gives generously to all without reproach, and it will be given him." So pray for God's wisdom about committing to a relationship. Too often, we don't pray because we don't want God's wisdom; we want our flesh—our fears and desires—to guide our decision. But how foolish this is! Go to God in prayer; tell him why you want to commit to a certain man or woman (or why you are afraid to). Ask him to let you trust him first, and then, based on faith, decide what to do.

The third tool is accountability. Ask that trusted adviser not merely to give you counsel, but also to challenge you to do the right thing and to act on the right convictions. This is what friends are for—not to mention parents and pastors! If you want to act rightly, becoming accountable is always a great help.

He Said, She Said

Before moving on from the topic of commitment, we need to remind the man that he has a responsibility to clarify this matter with the woman. Remember from the teaching in Genesis 2 that a godly man is to nurture and protect. In dating, this means to nurture and protect her heart. One of the chief ways a man does this is by initiating and welcoming conversations about where he and the woman are together. The lack of clarity regarding commitment causes many women to suffer. The man is not obliged to commit to a particular woman, but he is obliged to be clear and honest about his commitment. The woman, of course, is not obliged to accept a man's offer of commitment. She may think that he is moving too fast and that a lower level of commitment is better. The point is that for a dating relationship to be healthy, the commitment level must be defined and understood, and it is a Christian man's duty to take the lead in this. In so doing, he will gain the trust and respect of the woman he is dating; indeed, it is precisely by his unwillingness to address commitment issues that so many Christian men earn the suspicion and contempt of godly women and sour otherwise promising relationships.

> A godly man is to nurture and protect.
> In dating, that means to nurture
> and protect the woman's heart.

Moreover, by its definition, commitment should never be coerced; to be real, it must be freely given. Coercion always produces resentment and resistance. A woman should not complain to or manipulate a man to make commitments to her. But she is both wise and right to expect a clear definition of commitment and to respond accordingly. This is where perhaps a majority of dating relationships go down the tubes: the man never wants to "talk about the relationship," usually because he wants to enjoy the woman's intimacy without the burden of commitment. The woman begins to lose her trust in him, but since she wants to get married, she starts manipulating him to make a commitment. Once this point is reached, the relationship is practically sunk. We have often advised women (and sometimes men) in this situation to exit the relationship immediately, thus probably saving themselves at least a year of wasted emotional anguish. It is just this simple: if a man is not willing to assume his responsibility for a woman's emotional care, and thus resents talking about commitment, then he should not be trusted with a woman's precious heart. Sadly, this describes legions of men today—even Christian men and those who are well into their thirties and beyond. Until a man is ready to assume responsibility for a woman's heart—and that demands willingness to give and to define commitment— then he should not toy with the emotions of his sisters in Christ and should not be encouraged to enter into or remain in a dating relationship.

When the man refuses to "talk about the relationship" and the woman starts manipulating to gain commitment— break up immediately!

So what does a woman do when a man is unwilling to show commitment? She should remember that the level of commitment defines the amount of intimacy that may be safely enjoyed. In short, a man should not be permitted to have his cake and eat it, too, all at the woman's emotional expense! Intimacy follows commitment, and a woman should not offer increased intimacy—time spent together, sharing of the heart, little acts of helping ministry—without increased commitment from the man. Far too many women conclude that the way to win more commitment is to give more and more intimacy. This is a perilous mistake, both for the woman and for the relationship. We have sometimes referred to this as the "spirit of harlotry." It may involve yielding to a man's sexual advances or just baking cookies for him. There is a big difference between the two, but the spirit is the same: the woman thinks that she has to sell herself to gain the love of a man. Instead, a Christian woman should look to God to provide for her needs and show the self-respect that demands a man to step forward in commitment before she steps out into new intimacy.

> Many women seek to gain commitment
> by giving intimacy. This "spirit of harlotry"
> is wrong for any Christian woman.

Commitment is a major issue in many dating relationships because it is an indicator of a man's and a woman's readiness to take on the responsibilities of marriage. Until a man and woman have knelt before God, opened their hearts, and asked God to give them grace to meet the demands of biblical masculinity and femininity, then they are not ready to move beyond friendly acquaintances into a dating relationship.

8

Could This Be Love?

From Dating to Marriage

"You've Got Mail." "Yes." "Those are very power-ful words." "Yes!" Thus spoke Tom Hanks to Meg Ryan in the romantic comedy *You've Got Mail.* There is a reason why this story struck a chord with millions of moviegoers. It tells of two strangers who meet on the Internet and begin sharing their hearts. In real life they are bitter competitors. His big bookstore chain puts her neighborhood book-shop out of business; he is attracted to her and feels sorry, while she simply hates his guts. But all the while, unbe-knownst to them, their minds and hearts are anonymously becoming one in the safe confines of cyberspace. They share their hopes and dreams, their fears and frustrations, their triumphs and calamities in a way they've never been able to do in a flesh-and-blood relationship.

Why were "You've Got Mail" such powerful words? Why were e-mail messages able to unite two people who didn't even know that they knew each other? The reason is that through their online messages, they had opened themselves up to each other. They had ministered to the needs of each other's hearts. They had shared themselves in exchanges that were intimate—not physically intimate but emotionally and intellectually intimate. That is how they so grew in their love that when they actually met, their prior problems fell completely away.

Now, we are not advocating e-mail dating as the answer to our problems! But *You've Got Mail* connects us back to an earlier, more elegant age, a time when men and women exchanged letters and spent afternoons walking in the park. Many couples experience this today through long phone conversations in which they talk about nothing and everything for hours. There is something to this, because it is the sharing of our minds and our hearts that makes us one and causes our love to grow.

Growing (Not Falling) in Love

So far, we have observed that as the relationship grows, the level of commitment needs to be defined and that the man should take responsibility for this, while a woman responds in terms of the intimacy she offers. If we have one message in this book, it is this matter of the need for commitment and intimacy, along with interdependence, to be kept in line. This is also how we got the book's title. A close friend of ours was relating her anguish in dating, precisely because of undefined commitment and intimacy. She told us that as they were walking along, the man suddenly grasped her hand. Now they were holding hands! In his fuzzy male brain, the only thoughts were those of warmth and pleasure: "Ah, to hold a woman's hand! What joy!" But her mind was filled with questions and anxiety.

She told us, "When a man holds my hand, I want to know what he means!" And she was right! Therefore, we say, "You're not just holding hands; you're holding hearts!"

Because of the way God made them, women understand this immediately. But men often do not. Intimacy demands an accounting in terms of commitment! A healthy, growing dating relationship is one in which the two are clearly defined and faithfully respected, giving honor to God and loving our neighbor as ourselves.

This is the key to "the dating game," which is no game at all. Most dating relationships will pass through stages that draw closer to marriage. There is the first date (commitment, intimacy, and interdependence are low!). Then a couple is dating, and commitment is defined, even if it is tentative. They will agree to get together at certain intervals, to talk on the phone, and to pray for each other. Before long, they should agree to meet each other's friends and families, and perhaps to attend church together. They may help each other to buy a computer or a car. They may make dinners for each other. As the relationship grows, they will begin sharing interests. One may be a tennis player, so the other takes lessons. Since one of them loves classical music, the other will read a book on Mozart and go to the symphony. Their lives will become increasingly interdependent, as they learn to share each other's activities and become known to colleagues at work and a broader circle of friends, and as they engage in a higher degree of personal ministry to each other. This is the process of leaving and cleaving that Genesis 2:24 talks about, and it normally does not happen all at once. At a certain point, a couple will find themselves discussing the prospect of marriage. Again, it is the man who should bring this up; or if the woman wants to talk about it, the man should be willing, candid, and honest. In our case, we reached the point where we began talking about marriage and discussing things such as our desire for children and ideas of child-raising. We shared our willingness and desire for the relationship to progress to marriage at some time, but also agreed that we were not yet at that point.

> As the relationship grows, they will begin sharing interests and their lives will become increasingly interdependent.

The point is that at each step of the way, the relationship grows in terms of commitment, intimacy, and interdependence. For most couples, it will be not long after talking about marriage in positive terms that the time will come for a marriage engagement. This is an important topic worthy of its own discussion (see page 153). Engagement is a special time that must be handled purposefully. Deciding to marry and planning a marriage will probably be the first big decisions you will make together. At this point, a relationship begins taking on some (but not all!) of the characteristics of marriage.

> The relationship grows in terms of commitment, intimacy, and interdependence.

What about Sex?

By now, most readers will have wondered how sex fits into the picture. So let's not wait any longer to address the subject. It is here that any Christian idea of dating and the world's ideas clash most directly. In today's society, intimacy means practically nothing more than having sex. Couples meet and immediately begin enjoying sexual intercourse, committed either to immoral hedonism or to the idea that sex will serve as the foundation for love. This goes a long way toward explaining why so many marriages, built on no stronger foundation than sexual thrills, end in divorce soon after the flames of passion have died down.

One reason why couples are tempted to engage in premarital sex is that their bodies drive them in that direction. In the right setting—that is, marriage—sex is a wonderful gift from God. Sex is given for our good. But God gave sex to be the servant of love and never the slave of lust. God intends for love to express itself in the commitment of marriage, and only then for intimacy to unite us in the joys of sexual love.

The problem of many singles is not their sexual desires, but their unwillingness or inability to exercise the self-control necessary to guard the sanctity of marital love. The unbelieving world has given up on this altogether. Paul says that before being born again, "we all once lived in the passions of our flesh, carrying out the desires of the body" (Eph. 2:3). This being the case, it may be tragic that unbelieving people fall into immoral sex, but it is understandable. Not so for Christians! Yes, Christians still struggle with the passions of the flesh, but we are empowered by God's Holy Spirit to live above the temptation to sin. In Christ, we are now "created after the likeness of God in true righteousness and holiness" (Eph. 4:24). Therefore, for Christians to dishonor our relationships with premarital sex is not only tragic but foolish in the extreme. It involves sin of a very high order and undermines the dignity and the purity of the love that God intends between a Christian man and woman.

So why do Christians fall into sexual sin? They let their guard down. They toy with it. Some think it is not altogether bad to sin this way. They don't understand that their sinful sexual experiences will come with them into marriage. So let's be clear about God's standards as expressed in the Bible: "Let marriage be held in honor among all, and let the marriage bed be undefiled, for God will judge the sexually immoral and adulterous" (Heb. 13:4). When a Christian couple falls into sexual sin, they should confess their sin to God and to each other, seek forgiveness in Jesus Christ, and repent in such a way that will result in a renewed commitment to obedience.

> Christians who fall into sexual sin should confess their sin to God, seek forgiveness in Christ, and repent in a renewed commitment to obedience.

A typical mistake made by Christian singles is to ask, "How far can we go?" The very question reveals a troubling attitude, and the one who asks it has already gone too far. But since it is the question that many really want to ask, this is an honest response to the Bible's teaching: "Not very far at all." Physical, sexual interaction between a man and a woman is reserved for marriage. Too many Christians believe that so long as full-blown sexual intercourse is resisted, other forms of sexual interaction are acceptable. But such an attitude is far out of line with the Bible. Let's look at some relevant passages.

In 1 Thessalonians 4:3–5, the apostle Paul writes, "For this is the will of God, your sanctification: that you abstain from sexual immorality; that each one of you know how to control his own body in holiness and honor, not in the passion of lust like the Gentiles who do not know God." This statement is very telling when it comes to Christians and sexuality. Paul is not saying that sex is bad, but that Christians are commanded by God to "abstain from sexual immorality." This refers to sexual interaction outside of marriage. Furthermore, Paul indicates the attitude that Christians ought to have toward sexual purity. Should we "go as far as we can" without getting into trouble? That is how unbelieving people think, as Paul describes them, "the Gentiles who do not know God." Those who know God realize that he calls for purity, and therefore we are to cultivate self-control, especially in our sexuality: "that each one of you know how to control his own body in holiness and honor." These are concepts that the world has long forgotten—holiness and honor. But Christians are to realize that our bodies belong to God and are themselves part of Christ's own Body (see 1 Cor. 6:13–17). Therefore, we treat ourselves and other Christians as objects worthy of holiness and honor. Paul goes on to say in this passage, "For God has not called us for impurity, but in holiness. Therefore whoever disregards this, disregards not man but God, who gives his Holy Spirit to you" (1 Thess. 4:7–8). This is the attitude we are to cultivate: sexual self-control so as to offer our bodies to God in holiness and honor.

It is noteworthy that the passage above involves something of a translation controversy. What the English Standard Version translates as "control his own body" is literally, in the Greek, "possess his own vessel." Some scholars think Paul means not control of one's own body but the proper taking of another's body, namely, a wife's. Under this view (the English Standard Version and some others provide it in a marginal note), the verse would read, "That you abstain from sexual immorality, that each one of you know how to take a wife for himself." If we consider both of these possible renderings, the point is very consistent with the Bible's overall teaching: God calls us to personal holiness, and this especially affects our sexuality, demanding self-control outside of marriage or the taking of a wife so as to enjoy sex in a holy and honorable way.

> God calls us to sexual holiness:
> this demands self-control outside of marriage
> or the taking of a wife to enjoy sex
> in a holy and honorable way.

The message to Christian singles is clear: God calls you to abstain from sex, not to toy with it. In doing so, you cultivate a holy relationship that is pleasing to God, and you give honor to yourself and your partner. If you find it necessary to engage in sex, you should get married— marriage being the God-given relationship in which sex is safe and appropriate.[1]

We should also note that Paul's teaching here is most specifically directed to men, and it is the Christian man who is called by God to take the lead in the sexual purity of the dating relationship, just as in issues of commitment and intimacy generally. In this way, a man begins loving his bride as Christ loved the church, presenting her undefiled to the Lord (Eph. 5:25–27).

When you start looking up New Testament passages calling for sexual purity, you realize how frequently this subject comes up in the writings of the apostles, and especially the apostle Paul. The early church began in a pagan and sexually debauched culture—one very much like the one we live in today. For Paul, a Christian witness was worth very little unless it was accompanied by personal godliness. In his sexually debauched culture, that meant sexual purity. Consider what he wrote to the Ephesians:

> But sexual immorality and all impurity or covetousness must not even be named among you, as is proper among saints. . . . For you may be sure of this, that everyone who is sexually immoral or impure, or who is covetous (that is, an idolater), has no inheritance in the kingdom of Christ and God." (Eph. 5:3–5)

These words show that immoral sex is not the only sin that the Bible cares about; Paul mentions covetousness here just as he condemns all sorts of other sins elsewhere. But we should not fail to notice the place of precedence given to sexual sin. You will find that Paul generally mentions it first when he lists condemned sins (see also 1 Cor. 6:9–10; Gal. 5:19–21; Col. 3:5–6). He is emphatic about the need for sexual purity for those who hope to inherit God's kingdom. Paul is not saying that a true believer will be eternally condemned for falling into sexual sin; as his writings abundantly emphasize, we are justified by grace alone through faith in Christ. But he is saying—emphatically so—that a truly saved person will not continue in a sexually immoral lifestyle. "You may be sure of this," he emphasizes, that a person who is characterized by sexual immorality is not going to enter into heaven because such a person cannot possibly be a genuine Christian. Far from inviting us to play around as much as possible and as close to the fire as we can without getting burned, Paul makes it clear that a sincere Christian will cultivate the highest moral and sexual purity, as essential to his or her worship of God.

A sincere Christian will cultivate the highest moral and sexual purity, as essential to his or her worship of God.

Single adults are bound to struggle with their sex drive. But the Bible does not respond to this by saying, "Well, then, go ahead and fool around a little!" The Bible's answer is that we should become married. Paul writes, "To the unmarried and the widows I say that it is good for them to remain single as I am. But if they cannot exercise self-control, they should marry. For it is better to marry than to be aflame with passion" (1 Cor. 7:8–9; see also v. 36). Speaking of our sex life, Paul says, "So glorify God in your body" (1 Cor. 6:19). People with the gift of singleness (little sex drive) should remain single and thus glorify God. All others should marry, and in the meantime or while God's providence rules otherwise, they are to honor God in their bodies by self-control in sexual purity.

Lust is a big problem with which many singles wrestle. Many men are thereby enmeshed in pornography. In this way they seek to gratify their sex drive without the inconvenience of loving a real person or sacrificing anything of themselves. A shocking number of Christian singles dishonor God through such sexual immorality, so that God is angered, the Holy Spirit is grieved, and our witness to the dying world is greatly damaged. According to God's Word, what these men need to do is to get married. This is God's provision for a healthy sex drive. While single they are called to resist temptation and to pursue marriage, which is God's provision for us.

> When Christian singles are sexually immoral, God is angered, the Holy Spirit is grieved, and our witness to the world is damaged.

The problem is that many singles—again, especially men—are simply too selfish, spiritually immature, or emotionally wounded to step forward into marriage. Therefore, huge numbers of godly women struggle with an unfulfilled, God-given desire for marriage. What God wants is for these needs he has given us—sex being God's gift to unite a man and a woman—to motivate us toward marriage. The answer for a great many single Christians today is to move past their selfishness, immaturity, and pain, to trust God and seek his grace to be the man or woman God intends, and to enter into the covenant relationship of marriage. Marriage is never a cure all, and it guarantees happiness to no one. But it is God's provision for our need of companionship and for the fulfillment of the sexual desires God has given.

All of that was our first answer to the Christian who feels the need to toy with sexual intimacy. "How can I not dabble in sex, when I have these strong desires?" The first answer is that God wants many of you to get married, and if that requires you to grow up, so much the better. But while you are dating—ideally, in the hopes of marriage— how are you to avoid falling into sexual sin? The answer is this: while you struggle with unfulfilled sexual desires, the last thing you should do is to toy with them. Human sexuality operates on a positive-feedback system. Each stimulus is designed not to leave you satisfied but to increase your desire until you finally join in sexual intercourse. If a couple is alone in an apartment and they begin kissing, that activity is designed physically and emotionally to motivate them to go further. Sooner or later, they very likely will. How much more true is this when they begin caressing and engaging in sexual foreplay. The whole point of the fore is to lead to the play! It is very unlikely that a couple that starts down this road will not arrive at its destination. How many sincere, committed Christians end up in bed together, asking themselves afterwards, "How did this happen?" It happened when they started toying with sexual activity, which God has designed for marriage alone.

Do not toy with sexual desires.

For this reason, we counsel Christian singles not to permit themselves to be in compromising situations. We practice this principle in our marriage. Neither one of us will allow ourselves to be in a situation that could lead to adultery. Why? Because we don't want to commit adultery. We want to honor God and protect our marriage. As Hebrews 13:4 says, "Let marriage be held in honor among all, and let the marriage bed be undefiled." This happens long before any sheets are ruffled. Just as married couples honor God by protecting their union at all times, so do singles honor marriage by not even putting themselves in situations in which natural temptations can be acted upon.

Singles honor marriage by avoiding temptations. "Flee from sexual immorality" (1 Cor. 6:18).

150

The Bible is consistent and urgent in its appeals to this end. "Flee from sexual immorality," Paul urges in 1 Corinthians 6:18. The only way to handle sexual temptation is not to toy with it but to flee from it. We are to leave compromising situations, and like Joseph from the arms of Potiphar's wife, we are to do so immediately.

Likewise, we must not invite temptation. That means that a dating couple has no reason to be alone in an apartment, much less the bedroom, especially at tempting times such as the evening hours. Dating couples should not engage in activities proper only for married couples. We once advised a couple against going on an ocean cruise together. They assured us that they would not give in to temptation and that they had separate (though adjoining) rooms. We told them either to protect their relationship by returning their tickets or to save the money and get just one room! Sure enough, when they returned home they soon confessed that they had fallen into sexual sin. "How did this happen to us?" they cried. "When you bought the tickets," we replied. This is what Solomon was talking about when he wrote the proverb that asks, "Can a man scoop fire into his lap without his clothes being burned?" (Prov. 6:27, NIV). The answer is well known to all who have tried.

The best way to honor God in a dating relationship is to abstain from all sexual interaction. This will have the additional benefit of helping you to become serious about marriage sooner than you otherwise probably would. Moreover, it will gain for marital sex a quality of purity and joy that will enhance its pleasure and its ability to bring two hearts together in holy union.

Sexual sin will damage and often ruin a promising dating relationship. We have found that as soon as a couple becomes sexually involved, they cease developing other, more foundational forms of intimacy—the kinds of intimacy needed for a healthy marriage. After all, if you are sleeping together, you are not going to spend a lot of time in coffee shops discussing the majesty of God, sharing what your childhoods were like, or laughing at the shoes of people walking by. What you will do is quickly pay the tab, go to one of your bedrooms, and start making love. Sex is simply too powerful, and it especially overwhelms the flesh when it is made illicit. "Stolen water is sweet," says the seductress of Proverbs 9:17, whose chamber leads the foolish into "the depths of Sheol" (v. 18).

Sexual sin will damage and often ruin a promising relationship. It stops the development of emotional, intellectual, and spiritual intimacy.

Back in our chapter on commitment, we noted the "spirit of harlotry" to which so many women are tempted. This is the message that women receive from billboards, magazine ads, and television as they grow up in our society: Their value as human beings, says the message, is precisely equal to their sensual appeal. Sadly, this message is often reinforced in the church, since sex appeal gains more attention than godliness. The result is that women are tempted to cultivate not the spiritual beauty of the inner self that is precious to God (1 Peter 3:4) but the broken-hearted sensuality of the harlot.

This is the final reason why Christians should abstain from all sexual interaction: because of the blessing it will be to the heart of the woman. It is not that she is not sexually tempted. Women are sexually tempted, only in a way that men do not experience. Sin tells the man that he can taste from the cookie jar. But sin tells a woman that she has to sell herself to be loved. A Christian man who takes the lead in sexual purity, and who tells the woman that her heart means more to him than her body, and her purity is more valuable to him than his own pleasure, liberates her from a cruel bondage and gives her a blessing that words can hardly describe. As one Christian woman told us, "You don't have to kiss me to know my character." A man who puts a woman's heart first can wonderfully show it by preserving her character instead of pursuing her for sexual pleasure.

So How Do You Know?

We believe that even in our sex-obsessed age, when love has been lost if not forgotten, Christians committed to a godly pattern of life can date both wholesomely and successfully. This means that sooner or later, one final matter will come up. It is an issue over which many stumble and for which biblical wisdom is greatly desired: "So how do I know if he or she is the one?"

Perhaps the biggest reason for the anguish that many feel at this point comes from the burden to find exactly the right partner for life. On the one hand, there is a great deal of wisdom behind this anxiety. This is an important decision! But on the other hand, the normal anxiety is often heightened by unhelpful and unrealistic expectations. The fact is that there is no perfect person for you to marry, and if someone were perfect they should never marry someone like you! There is no other kind of person for you to marry than a flawed sinner in need of God's grace and of a loving companion to walk together with in life. So put your checklist away and examine your attitude in the light of God's Word.

Normal anxiety about marriage is often heightened by unhelpful and unrealistic expectations. There is no perfect person for you to marry.

Many Christians think they are required to find "that one person" whom God has chosen for them in order to be happily married. It is certainly true that the God who ordains all things has also ordained the one person you will marry. But God does not tell you who that is beforehand. God does not expect us to plumb his secret will with supernatural knowledge, but rather to exercise our responsibility in a godly and obedient way. We know that God forbids a believer to marry a nonbeliever (1 Cor. 7:39; 2 Cor. 6:14). A woman should not marry a man to whom she is not willing to submit, since God will require this of her (Eph. 5:22–24; 1 Peter 3:1). A man should marry a woman only if he is willing to show her the self-sacrificing love modeled by Jesus Christ on the cross (Eph. 5:25). But within biblical boundaries such as these, Christians should feel a great deal of freedom and should have confidence that God's grace will enable them to love another in marriage.

In other words, what matters most is not finding the one right person but becoming the person that God wants you to be. Before judging the man or woman you are with—scrutinizing and appraising every attribute and characteristic, as if you were buying a horse—you ought instead to scrutinize your own heart. Here are some questions to ask before an engagement to marriage:

1. What would it mean for me to love him or her in accordance with the Bible's teaching?
2. Am I willing to commit myself to anyone "for better or for worse, for richer or for poorer, in sickness and in health?"
3. Can I be steadfast in fidelity and servant-hearted in ministry?
4. Is God leading our lives in similar directions?
5. Do we have similar goals and ideas about children?

The issue is not whether you can find someone worthy of your love, but whether you are ready to give a love that is worthy of marriage. And if not, then you should turn to God and ask, "Why not?" God says that it is not good for man to be alone, and this means that we are to learn to love in the way that marriage requires.

> What matters most is not finding
> the right person, but being the right person—
> the person that God wants you to be.

This raises the issue of compatibility. A great many Christian books and counselors hail compatibility as the key to a successful and happy marriage. In our view, this reflects the consumer model of our secular culture more than the sacrificial model found in Holy Scripture. Marriage, experts tell us, works only when our needs and desires are met. But no such teaching is found in the Bible. In Scripture, we find that marriage works as a man and a woman stand before God in obedient faith, giving instead of taking, and serving instead of demanding. This is our problem with the emphasis on finding a compatible companion: it turns the whole of the Christian life on its head. Jesus said of himself, "The Son of Man came not to be served but to serve" (Matt. 20:28), and surely marital love can be built on no other foundation.

> Marriage works as a man and woman stand before God in obedient faith, giving instead of taking, and serving instead of demanding.

This does not mean that you should seek to honor God by marrying someone you find totally unattractive. But there are several reasons why we counsel couples not to be overly focused on compatibility. The first is that it directs us to a selfish rather than a servant attitude toward marriage. But second, the fact is that a dating couple will seldom be able to accurately assess the other person. For instance, go out and find a married couple who have been together for ten years or so. Ask them from their present perspective how much they knew about each other before they were married. They will tell you that they knew very little! We can honestly tell you that the great majority of what we now know about each other (having been married now for twelve years) we learned after we were married. Before marriage, we didn't live together. We didn't share one income and a home. We weren't raising children. We weren't ministering to each other sexually. We were not yoked together for life. Before marriage, it is simply not possible for most of us to know what we will know only after our lives have been joined as one.

156

So how do you know whether you are compatible or not? It is one thing to both enjoy playing tennis. But how do you respond when a two-year-old vomits on you? How will you get along on two hours of sleep a night when you have a difficult baby, or when you learn that you will not be able to have children together? How will you work together when the woman leaves the workplace to be a mother and changes cities for the husband's job transfer? How will you react when her mother moves in for you to take care of her or when one of you is paralyzed in an accident? Few of us will be able to assess our compatibility in the face of these challenges while dating, but these are the things that a lifetime of marriage entails. We are sorry if this is shocking, but compatibility had better not be the key to marriage, or else our happiness depends on a shot in the dark.

Third, to most of us, finding a compatible mate means having a marriage that requires minimal change from us. We are selfish and lazy, especially when it comes to character change, so we want someone who will fit nicely just as we are. But what makes us think this is what God desires? Part of what made Eve a "suitable helper" for Adam was that she was *not* just like him. The love that God wants us to practice is self-sacrificing love—it is *this* that many of us find incompatible with our present lifestyles. "This is the will of God, your sanctification," wrote Paul (1 Thess. 4:3). For too many, the search for a compatible mate is really a determination to avoid sanctification.

So compatibility is *not* the key to marriage. What, then, if not compatibility, should we consider when asking, "Is he or she a person I can marry?" We suggest that there are a number of matters about which you can, indeed, make a confident decision and that truly are essential for a dating relationship to enter into a loving and godly marriage.

Compatibility is *not* the key to marriage.
God wants us to practice self-sacrificing love.

The first is this: "Knowing what I do about this person, is he or she genuinely committed to God through faith in Christ and earnestly determined to live in obedience to the Bible?" It is our conviction, based on experience in ministry and on God's Word, that two Christians who share an attraction, who are committed in faith to God through Christ, and who are determined to obey the Bible's teachings will be able to love each other in marriage. The problem we face is that we don't know how to love, but God teaches us to love through his Word. The following passage from the apostle John was not written directly about marriage, but it might as well have been:

> Beloved, let us love one another, for love is from God. . . . In this is love, not that we have loved God but that he loved us and sent his Son to be the propitiation for our sins. Beloved, if God so loved us, we also ought to love one another. . . . God is love, and whoever abides in love abides in God, and God abides in him. By this is love perfected with us. . . . We love because he first loved us. (1 John 4:7–19)

So the key question is this: "Is this person really abiding in God and bearing positive spiritual fruit?" Until you are confident of an answer to that question, you should rightly be nervous about making the commitment that marriage demands. None of us is perfect in our discipleship to Christ, and for most of us marriage itself will move us forward greatly in our walk with God. But the essential question is whether or not you have confidence that this is a person redeemed by the blood of Jesus Christ, growing in grace through the indwelling power of the Holy Spirit, and genuinely committed to biblical obedience as a pattern of life. If that describes the man or woman with whom you are considering marriage, it is a very good sign that God will give you what it takes to love each other.

Is he or she genuinely committed to God and determined to obey the Bible? Is this person abiding in God and bearing spiritual fruit?

One particular issue that is important for marriage is how you communicate and respond to conflict. A healthy marriage requires good communication, especially when it comes to feelings, expectations, and concerns. Can you and your potential spouse talk openly about difficult matters, without becoming defensive or hostile? Coupled with this is your reaction to conflict. In a world like ours, it is simply impossible for two sinners to live in close contact without conflict. All marriages experience conflict, and our response to it determines to a great degree whether or not we will experience harmony and peace. Here are some questions regarding how your partner handles conflict: Does he or she listen or simply dictate and demand? Is he or she harsh or mean-spirited when angry? Does he or she become easily angered and defensive when confronted with problems?

Then there are these essential matters that will exert a tremendous influence on your ability to live in harmony:

1. Is he or she willing to repent when his or her sins are pointed out?
2. Is he or she willing and eager to forgive your sins?
3. Does conflict resolve itself in reconciliation and a new determination to obey God?
4. Is he or she willing to commit to you based on the biblical standard of what God requires?
5. Is he willing to love you as Christ loves the church? Is she willing to honor and respect you in the Lord?

These are things that a couple should talk about, pray about to God, and strive for together if they are hoping to be happily married. Repentance, forgiveness, and new obedience, all through faith in Jesus Christ, are the actions of godly love in marriage, and a commitment to them should be evident before an engagement to marriage.

Is he or she defensive in communications? Is he or she mean-spirited or angry when confronted with problems? Is he or she willing to repent and eager to forgive?

Suppose you have soberly and prayerfully concluded that the person you love is sincerely committed to God through faith in Christ, is growing spiritually, and is resolved to obey God's Word. Suppose, as well, that you are making real progress in communicating to each other about your interactions, and that you are learning to respond to conflict with repentance, forgiveness, and new obedience. In that case, there is really only one question for you to ask: Are you prepared to accept the obligations of marriage and to love and serve as God will call you in marriage to this person? If not, then ask yourself, "Why not?" Every Christian should seek to learn how to love, just as we are called to learn how to rely on the Lord in faith. If so—if you are willing to commit yourself to this person in reliance on God and following his Word—then despite all of your failings and his or hers, by God's grace you can look forward to a marriage relationship in which your obedience is blessed. Notice that we have not included matters such as how much money you have saved up, what your job situation is like, or how far along you are in school. God works within the midst of any given circumstances, and Christians should strive to allow God, rather than circumstances, to rule their lives.

Are you prepared to love and serve
as God calls for in marriage? If not, why not?

If you are still wavering, then ask yourself this: "How do I feel about walking away from this relationship?" Ask: "Has God so knit our affections that I can hardly imagine not sharing my life with him or her?" These questions will often help us to discover the real state of our hearts. Then ask, "What do I think life is about, if not serving God as I learn how to love and to trust him through a marriage union to another sincere Christian?" Are you deterred from marriage by selfish delusions of freedom—as if an inability to love were any kind of real freedom—or by an idolatrous desire for success or money or fame? As the Bible tells it, God has designed us to live together as man and woman, and his provision for our nurture and care—physically, emotionally, spiritually, and sexually—is marriage.

Obviously, a decision to pursue marriage is a serious and even a daunting thing. Not every couple who dates will find it wise to advance into the covenant of marriage, nor should they. Ultimately, such a question as "Should I marry this person?" can be answered only through prayer for God's wisdom, through reflection on God's Word, and through a serious examination of your own heart. But Christians should do all of these things with confidence in God's ability to help them to love and to bless them through marriage with a godly partner whom they have come to know, to trust, and to love.

9

Waiting for Love?

AS WE CONCLUDE THIS BOOK, we know that many of you are not currently in a dating relationship. You may not even be aware of anyone who might be a suitable mate. No doubt this is a significant source of anxiety and, for some, even of despair. We wrote this as a biblical how-to book for dating. But one of the most important issues is the very opposite: how to *not* be dating.

The "Gift" of Singleness

We know very well one piece of advice that many will have received from other Christians. It goes like this: "Singleness is a gift, so learn to rejoice in this gift God has given you." We want to pull our hair out every time we hear it. This has become something of a pet peeve with us in our ministry to so many dearly beloved single Christians because it is *not* true. For the vast majority of adult Christians, singleness is not a gift.

To be sure, the Bible speaks of the gift of singleness. But if you are reading this book—and especially if you are *still* reading it—you obviously do not have this gift! The apostle Paul speaks of the gift of singleness in 1 Corinthians 7: "I wish that all were as I myself am. But each has his own gift from God, one of one kind and one of another" (1 Cor. 7:7). It is perfectly clear in context that Paul is talking about the glorious gift of a lack of sex drive. The verses before and after speak of marriage as God's provision for the healthy human sex drive, the exception to which is the gift of singleness that Paul has and wishes that you had, too. You know if you have it or not. Not many of us do. Paul assures us that it is a great gift (although, frankly, we cannot work up much envy for him).

We have known a few Christians who had this gift of singleness. They didn't think romantically about others of the opposite sex, and there was nothing wrong or perverse about them. They did not struggle with lust, either. There are people with this gift, and in our experience it is usually someone called to a particular and intense ministry. But there are not many such people. For the rest of you, singleness is not a gift, and it would be nice if people stopped saying that it is.

So if singleness is not a gift, what is it? Singleness is a trial. For many, it is a particularly intense trial and challenges their spiritual and emotional well-being. When it drags on for many years, it is a wearying trial. It is difficult and unpleasant, and we need to seek God's grace for this trial as with any other.

For the majority of adult Christians,
singleness is not a gift but a trial.

One thing this tells us is that our assertion in the first chapter of this book is true: it is good for adults to marry. Paul is quite blunt in 1 Corinthians 7:9: "It is better to marry than to be aflame with passion." But marriage is good for more than serving our sexual passion. Marriage is good for the intimate companionship between a man and a woman. Marriage is good for the mutual ministry and care we give and receive, and it is good because of the children whom God often brings into the world and the church through marriage. Therefore, whenever we hear that someone is "just looking for a spouse," we reply, "Bravo!" What a wise and natural thing for an adult man or woman to do. So long as we take out the "just"—as if seeking a spouse totally defined the person's life—we are always glad to encounter such biblically realistic Christians.

We have increasingly become pro-marriage in our ministry to singles, out of both personal experience and biblical conviction. We believe that Christian couples can love one another in the grace that God gives, no matter how incompatible they may seem. As we have said, the key to marriage is repentance, forgiveness, and renewed obedience—and if Christians can live in such a way, then they can be happily married. We have experienced this ourselves, despite our own hang-ups and sin, and we encourage singles to seek marriage for themselves.

But since marriage doesn't always happen and sometimes—increasingly, it seems—singleness can last a long time, let's consider this matter of its being a trial. Singleness involves loneliness, sexual frustration, and unfulfilled dreams. It is a difficult ordeal. But let's understand something about trials: everybody has them. Singleness may be a trial, but it is not the only trial. Married people have trials—lots of them, in fact. Parents

165

have loads of trials. When Jesus said, "In the world you will have tribulation" (John 16:33), he was talking to us all. So in dealing with singleness as a trial, we need to realize that singles are not the only people with trials and that curing singleness will not cure the problem of trials in this life.

Everyone has trials. Curing singleness
will not cure the problem of trials.

One thing this means to Christians struggling with singleness is that they must avoid envy of and resentment for those who are married. If needed, they should repent of such thoughts. It is so easy for long-single women to look upon married moms with resentment, as if their lives were just picture perfect. It may be true that another person has something that you want. But you may have something that she wants, too. The longer we serve in ministry, the more we see that pretty much everyone is envying everyone else. It really is pitiful. None of us has the circumstances we really want, and the circumstances we have always provide us with challenges. What a shame it is when we allow such envy and resentment to hinder the Christian fellowship that ought to be one of our chief blessings in this life.

Practically all the apostles wrote about trials. Peter said, "Beloved, do not be surprised at the fiery trial when it comes upon you to test you, as though something strange were happening to you. But rejoice insofar as you share Christ's sufferings, that you may also rejoice and be glad when his glory is revealed" (1 Peter 4:12–13). This passage tells us to expect trials, but more importantly that suffering is an important part of our discipleship with Christ. How we handle suffering and trials is an important indicator of the kind of Christians we are. Peter does not tell us to rejoice about our sufferings, but rejoice that we share suffering with Christ and that all our present difficulties will work together for our eternal glory. Paul concurred, writing in Philippians 1:29, "For it has been granted to you that for the sake of Christ you should not only believe in him but also suffer for his sake."

Peter also links trials to the refining of our faith. He observed in 1 Peter 1:6–7, "Now for a little while, if necessary, you have been grieved by various trials, so that the tested genuineness of your faith—more precious than gold that perishes though it is tested by fire may be found to result in praise and glory and honor at the revelation of Jesus Christ." The idea is that of refining our faith, the way a goldsmith refines raw gold. He cools and then super-heats the ore so that he can scrape away the dross. This is what God is doing to us in our trials, purifying the thing that we most need—our faith in him. Perhaps your frustrations in waiting for love are intended to draw you nearer to God and to teach you reliance on his grace.

Both the apostles Paul and James linked our trials with the cultivation of strong, godly character. Paul wrote, "We rejoice in our sufferings, knowing that suffering produces endurance, and endurance produces character, and character produces hope, and hope does not put us to shame, because God's love has been poured into our hearts through the Holy Spirit who has been given to us" (Rom. 5:3–5). James adds, "Count it all joy, my brothers, when you meet trials of various kinds, for you know that the testing of your faith produces steadfastness. And let steadfastness have its full effect, that you may be perfect and

167

complete, lacking in nothing" (James 1:2–4). Both apostles identify trials as producing steadfastness—a strong ability to endure under duress—which Paul says leads to character and character to hope. The key to our trials is to get out of them all that God intends for us—and in this we can rejoice.

God promised none of us carefree lives. What he promised is his faithfulness in forgiving our sins and preserving us through the trials of this world. It is because of God's merciful grace that Paul could rejoice, "This slight momentary affliction is preparing for us an eternal weight of glory beyond all comparison" (2 Cor. 4:17). What God is preparing for us through our trials is incomparably greater than the things we long for in this world. We would gladly settle for mere happiness in life. But God is determined that we should be holy, and through holiness partake of his own glory. It is for that cause that God ordains our trials in this life. Christians struggling with singleness, then, should not label their troubles a "gift." But they should realize that through their often painful trials, God is working an incomprehensible gift: eternal life and the hope of glory. Realizing this, we can rejoice in our trials and sufferings to the glory of God.

> The key to trials is to get out of them all that God intends for us.

The Rare Jewel of Contentment

So besides looking for a spouse, to what should Christian singles devote their energies? One essential answer is that we are to be cultivating the wonderful Christian grace of contentment. This is what Paul said about his own trials, writing in Philippians:

> I have learned in whatever situation I am to be content. I know how to be brought low, and I know how to abound. In any and every circumstance, I have learned the secret of facing plenty and hunger, abundance and need. I can do all things through him who strengthens me. (Phil. 4:11–13)

Notice that Paul said he had to learn "the secret" of contentment. It was not easy for him, but through God's strength he learned that he could "do all things." We think of that verse inspiring us to go for it in life or to accomplish something great. But the specific great thing that Paul meant was that we can be contented in every circumstance—including singleness—"through him who strengthens me."

One of our favorite books, and one that has made a lasting impression on both our lives and our marriage, is Jeremiah Burroughs's *The Rare Jewel of Christian Contentment*. Burroughs, a seventeenth-century English Puritan, wrote the book to expound on Paul's statements about contentment in Philippians 4. He described Christian contentment as "that sweet, inward, quiet, gracious frame of spirit, which freely submits to and delights in God's wise and fatherly disposal in every condition."[1] Note that the contentment to which God calls us is in "every condition." That includes singleness.

What Paul learned and what Burroughs wrote was that contentment does not arise from our circumstances. If we are ever to be content—and with contentment to have true joy—it will come only through our relationship with the Lord our God. According to Arthur Pink,

"Contentment, then, is the product of a heart resting in God. It is the soul's enjoyment of that peace that passes all understanding. It is the outcome of my will being brought into subjection to the Divine will. It is the blessed assurance that God does all things well, and is, even now, making all things work together for my ultimate good."[2]

> "Contentment . . . is the product
> of a heart resting in God."

With this in mind, we want to provide an unchanging rule for singles to remember, namely, *if you cannot be contented in singleness, you will not be contented in marriage.* Singleness is not something that keeps us from contentment and joy. Rather, it is a trying circumstance in which we are to look in faith to God, submitting in his good and sovereign will, and looking to him for every blessing. But singleness is not the only such trying circumstance. Another is called marriage, as two sinners seek to live in harmony without killing each other. Yet another trying circumstance is called *parenthood*, in which two exhausted sinners who seldom speak with each other seek to live in harmony with each other and a whole pack of other little sinners. In all these circumstances, the challenge is not to change the circumstances but to learn what Paul learned: "I know how to be brought low, and I know how to abound. In any and every circumstance, I have learned the secret of facing plenty and hunger, abundance and need. I can do all things through him who strengthens me" (Phil. 4:12–13).

> If you cannot be contented in singleness,
> you will not be contented in marriage.
> We *can* be content—through Christ!

We mean what we say here: we mean it as a warning and as a constructive challenge. If you are not able to be contented as a single, you will not be contented or joyful or fulfilled as a husband or wife. No one person can be the source of your contentment. Contentment comes only from God, and the sooner we start seeking it in him, the better off we will be. We have known many Christians who bitterly complained and anguished over their singleness. If only they could be married, then they would be happy. Time after time, we have found that when God blesses such a person with a flawed but perfectly suitable spouse, he or she is heard soon after the wedding—perhaps right after the honeymoon—complaining about the terrible burden imposed by his or her grossly inadequate mate. Likewise, we have known many Christians who expected to find all their happiness in parenthood. Raising children is a joy and delight—we praise the Lord for the blessing of our children—but if you seek your happiness in it alone, you will not be happy. Martyn Lloyd-Jones explains:

> Man's happiness was never meant to be determined by his circumstances, and that is the fatal blunder that we all tend to make. . . . Man's happiness depends on one thing only—and that is his relationship to God! . . . We cannot get it anywhere else. We must come back to the soul and to God who made it. We were made for him, we are meant for him, we have a correspondence with him, and we will never come to rest until, like that needle on

the compass, we strike that northern point, and there we come to rest—nowhere else.[3]

We earlier appealed to Psalm 16 to show how finding our joy in God empowers us to love one another in marriage. The same principle applies to singleness. David could exult, "Therefore my heart is glad" (Ps. 16:9), because in the preceding verses he said, "I bless the LORD" (Ps. 16:7). This shows that true worship is the cause of joy among God's people. But what enables such heart-exaltation of God? The answer is shown in verses 5–6, which speak of humble submission to God's good and holy pleasure in our lives: "The LORD is my chosen portion and my cup; you hold my lot. The lines have fallen for me in pleasant places; indeed, I have a beautiful inheritance." But where does such submission to God's will come from but a faith that realizes that it is better to be afflicted as God's people than to abound apart from him? "As for the saints in the land," David sings, "they are the excellent ones, in whom is all my delight" (Ps. 16:3). So in singleness and in marriage, faith leads us to submit to God's will, submission leads us to worship God, and worship leads us into joy. This pattern remains true today, and the rare jewel of Christian contentment is available to us in all our circumstances, including the trial of singleness, through a faith that submits to God's will and a heart that is lifted up in worship of him. The result is a deep, contented joy that is not of this world and that nothing can take away. David concludes, "You make known to me the path of life; in your presence there is fullness of joy; at your right hand are pleasures forevermore" (Ps. 16:11).

"You make known to me the path of life; in your presence there is fullness of joy" (Ps. 16:11).

Don't let the trial of singleness take away your joy as you exult in the Lord. We have occasionally needed to remind dear Christian singles that bitterness is not a fruit of the Holy Spirit. But joy is the fruit of God's presence; it flows from our relationship with the Lord, who redeemed us for eternal life in glory with him.

Psalm 37 provides wonderful encouragement to all of us who need help looking to God for all our needs. David reminds us, "Be still before the LORD and wait patiently for him" (Ps. 37:7). That is a great verse for all who look for fervently desired blessings. While you long for a spouse and while you act on that desire in prudent ways, allow God to decide the time and the manner of his answer. Be still before him and wait upon him, and you will be blessed.

Verse 4 puts this idea in especially wonderful terms: "Delight yourself in the LORD, and he will give you the desires of your heart." What could be more comforting than that? Having your heart's desires filled comes not by delighting in marriage or in some other worldly blessing. It comes by delighting in the Lord. In this way, we allow God to shape our desires in the manner in which he designed in order to fill them to the brim and overflowing.

Many are tempted to fret and even to sin in anxiety. But verse 8 warns us, "Refrain from anger, and forsake wrath! Fret not yourself; it tends only to evil." Above all, we must never envy unbelievers when they have things that we desire. "Better is the little that the righteous has than the abundance of many wicked. For the arms of the wicked shall be broken, but the LORD upholds the righteous" (Ps. 37:16–17). Instead, if you "wait for the LORD and keep his way," you can be sure that "he will exalt you to inherit the land" (Ps. 37:34). For all these reasons, God is the answer for all our needs, tenderly ministering to us with Fatherly love: "The salvation of the righteous is from the LORD; he is their stronghold in the time of trouble" (Ps. 37:39).

Servants of Christ

Finally, Christian singles, while acting in faith to seek a spouse, must make themselves useful to Christ and his church in every possible way. Singleness may not be a gift, but it certainly offers lots of time for most people. Use that time for the glory of God and the good of Christ's people. Singleness is particularly a time for service.

This means that if you have time, give it to Jesus. Devote yourself to studying his Word and to developing strong habits of prayer and worship. If you have gifts (and you do), use them for service in the church and for extending Christ's kingdom. People are perishing in sin with no one to tell them the gospel. Can you reach out to them? Can you extend a caring hand and a warm smile? Can you tell them the good news that Jesus came to redeem us from our sin?

If you have time, give it to Jesus. Study his Word and develop strong habits of prayer and worship. Use your gifts for service. Reach out to the lost. Extend a caring hand and a warm smile.

Too many singles think that life starts only with marriage. But singles must cultivate a purposeful life of Christian growth and service. You are not stuck in a holding pattern, just waiting to land at the great airport of life. The habits you develop as a single will carry over into marriage, and you will probably pass them on to your children. Remember, it is death—not a wedding—that removes every vestige of sin and presents us glorious before God. As singles, we must cultivate godly habits and the fruit of the Spirit that enables us to lead holy and effective lives. If you believe that God intends for you to be married, develop and cultivate habits that will benefit you in marriage, such as cooking, home repair, and financial management. We have often reminded lethargic, time-wasting Christians that even while they are single, and with perhaps no one to date in sight, they are nonetheless determining what kind of marriage they will have and are even raising their future children by the character and habits they are cultivating.

> The habits you develop as a single will carry over into marriage, and you may pass them on to your children.

We have been greatly blessed by Christian singles, and we know how mightily God can use them. We met in a Christian singles group at Rick's church. Rick was a new convert; he was baptized at a Christian singles retreat. Sharon was raised as a believer, but was greatly blessed there as well. When we think back to those last years of our single lives—Rick in his early 30s and Sharon in her mid-20s—what we remember is the passion for Christ, the devotion to godliness, and the thrill of worship that animated that singles group. Some of the believers who have most influenced and inspired us to wholehearted discipleship in the Lord Jesus were singles. We think back to those years and to that group, and we do not remember much about who was dating whom. We remember the Word we studied in our first Bible study together. We remember the examples of sacrificial service we encountered. And we remember the living faith that filled so many with contentment and joy, for all their trials and all the heartaches of singleness and dating. We humbly dedicate this book to them, some of whom have already gone ahead of us into heaven, in whose company we received not just the blessing of our marriage, but also the incalculable blessing of life-changing models of faith in Jesus Christ.

> Some of the Christians who most influenced
> and inspired us were singles.

We pray that these chapters have given you discernment from God's Word regarding dating and relationships, so that you might be blessed with healthy, loving, God-honoring marriages. But even more importantly than that, we pray that you will find your joy and salvation in the living Lord who alone can fill our souls, Jesus Christ.

> Trust in the LORD, and do good;
> > dwell in the land and befriend faithfulness.
> Delight yourself in the LORD,
> > and he will give you the desires of your heart.

Commit your way to the LORD;
    trust in him, and he will act.
He will bring forth your righteousness as the light,
    and your justice as the noonday.
Be still before the LORD and wait patiently for him. . . .
    (Ps. 37:3–7)

Notes

Chapter 1: Love Made New: God's Design in Creation

1. Walter Wangerin, *As For Me and My House* (Nashville: Nelson, 1999), 60–61.

2. Matthew Henry, *Commentary on the Whole Bible*, 6 vols. (Peabody, MA: Hendrickson, n.d.), 1:16.

Chapter 5: Words to the Wise: A Proverbial Take on Attraction

1. Lillian Glass, *The Complete Idiot's Guide to Understanding Men and Women* (Indianapolis: Alpha Books, 2000), 155.

Chapter 6: Table for Two: The First Date

1. Although many English versions translate 1 Corinthians 11:3 as "the head of a wife is her husband" (ESV), the Greek original is more general, saying simply, "The head of the woman is the man." In this case, the head of a married woman would be her husband, but the head of a single woman would be her father.

Chapter 8: Could This Be Love? From Dating to Marriage

1. In saying this, we should avoid the idea that if a couple has had sex, they are already married. This is nowhere taught in the Bible. Marriage is a covenant relationship that is consciously entered into. A sexually active dating couple has sinned against God and against each other. They are called to repentance and new obedience in the power of the Holy Spirit. They may realize that they ought to get married. But they are not married simply because they have had sex.

Chapter 9: Waiting for Love?

1. Jeremiah Burroughs, *The Rare Jewel of Christian Contentment* (Edinburgh: Banner of Truth, 1992), 19.

2. Arthur W. Pink, *Comfort for Christians* (Grand Rapids: Baker, 1989), 85–86.

3. D. Martyn Lloyd-Jones, *I Am Not Ashamed: Advice to Timothy* (Grand Rapids: Baker, 1996), 82–83.

Index of Scripture

Rick and Sharon Phillips met at a church singles group and were married twenty months later. After answering God's call to enter the ministry, Rick served as the pastor to the singles ministry in which they had met. Through their shared ministry to singles, they perceived a great need for clear biblical teaching on dating and singleness. The fruit of their ministry and of their love for singles is found in the pages of this book. They are the parents of five children and live in South Florida, where Rick is senior minister of First Presbyterian Church of Coral Springs/Margate, FL. He is co-editor of the Reformed Expository Commentary series and the author of numerous books on the Bible and Christian living, several of which feature discussion questions written by Sharon.